PRAISE FOR
Strength in Numbers: Collaborative Learning in Secondary Mathematics

Mathematics is a major barrier to the academic success of English language learners and students from historically marginalized racial and ethnic groups. This incisive, informative, well-researched, and practical book describes ways in which teachers can use collaborative learning to create secondary mathematics classrooms in which all students have an equal opportunity to learn. This book is a significant contribution to the literature on ways to close the achievement gap and to structure equal-status classrooms in secondary mathematics. It deserves a wide audience—including teachers, teacher educators, administrators, and policy makers.

—James A. Banks
Kerry and Linda Killinger Endowed Chair in Diversity Studies
and Director of the Center for Multicultural Education
University of Washington, Seattle

Strength in Numbers addresses two crucial problems in education and demonstrates how they are fundamentally related. The first is how to teach mathematics ambitiously; that is, how to engage all classroom learners in meaningful mathematics. The second is how to structure teaching so that teachers play a major role in improving the practice. Horn has done a beautiful job of grounding the relationship between these two challenges in real stories of teaching and teacher learning. The evidence for Horn's argument is strong, clearly presented, and broadly inclusive of the most important research on student and teacher learning.

—Magdalene Lampert
Professor of Education and Coordinator of the
Learning in, from, and for Teaching Practice Project
University of Michigan

Students talking and working together in groups, taking risks, joyful in learning, believing in their own smartness and that of their peers—for many teachers, this describes the kind of equitable math classroom that made us want to become educators. But how do we get there? Building on the efforts of teachers striving for just such classrooms, Horn offers practical principles, strategies, and insights that come straight from working in public, urban high schools. Mathematics teachers committed to group work, equitable participation, and building vibrant classroom communities should start here.

—Carlos Cabana
High School Mathematics Teacher
and Complex Instruction Educator

Horn makes a valuable contribution to the literature on equity in mathematics education. Drawing on her experiences as a teacher, researcher, and teacher educator, as well as the voices of classroom teachers, Horn constructs a compelling argument for collaborative learning for fostering equitable mathematics teaching. Recognizing that organizing groups for equity is not easy, she provides tools to help teachers minimize negative status effects that may emerge so all students can display their mathematical competencies. This book will prove to be a valuable resource for any teacher, teacher educator, or researcher in mathematics education concerned with designing equitable learning environments.

—Danny Bernard Martin
Professor of Mathematics Education and Mathematics
University of Illinois at Chicago

Strength in Numbers is a wonderful resource for all those who want their students to enjoy math through working with others. It includes all the details that are needed to put a highly effective and rare approach to group work into effect, and along the way includes many practical tidbits from a range of highly successful teachers. Group work often fails in classrooms because it is not equitable and some students do too much or too little work. This book outlines an *equitable* approach to group work that has been proven to work for students across the achievement range. We now live in a world in which collaboration is key to success, making this book a must-read for math teachers of all levels.

—Jo Boaler
Professor of Mathematics Education
Stanford University

This book describes in accessible yet vivid language what teachers can do to enhance mathematical discourse among students in diverse classrooms where students might have a wide range of previous academic achievement. Based on the highly successful practice of a group of teachers and the theoretically solid and empirically supported principles of complex instruction, the book will be a valuable resource for mathematics teachers at all grade levels.

—Rachel Lotan
Director of the Stanford Teacher Education Program (STEP)
Director of the Program for Complex Instruction
Stanford University

How do we teach more students harder mathematics—equitably? In this book, teacher, researcher, and teacher educator Lani Horn shows us how teachers can use collaborative learning techniques to engage and support their students in deep mathematical sense making. When things go right, there is true synergy, or, in other words: *Strength in Numbers*. Using compelling vignettes backed up by research, Horn shows how we can use the techniques of complex instruction to help more students grapple successfully with conceptually rich mathematics. The techniques illustrated in this book will help us move toward more equitable and mathematically powerful classrooms.

—Alan Schoenfeld
Elizabeth and Edward Conner Professor of Education
Graduate School of Education
University of California, Berkeley

Strength in Numbers

Collaborative Learning in Secondary Mathematics

Ilana Seidel Horn
Vanderbilt University's Peabody College
Nashville, Tennessee

NATIONAL COUNCIL OF
TEACHERS OF MATHEMATICS

more4u
www.nctm.org/more4u
Access code: SNC13791

Library of Congress Cataloging-in-Publication Data

Horn, Ilana Seidel.
  Strength in numbers : collaborative learning in secondary mathematics / Ilana
Seidel Horn.
    p. cm.
  Includes bibliographical references.
  ISBN 978-0-87353-663-9
  1. Mathematics--Study and teaching. 2. Group work in education. 3. Effective
teaching. 4. Classroom management. I. Title.
  QA20.G76H67 2011
  510.71'2--dc23
                        2011035296

The National Council of Teachers of Mathematics advocates for
high-quality mathematics teaching and learning for each and every student.

Printed in the United States of America

Contents

For Adam, Naomi, Elinor, and Judah,
who give me courage and humility

Introduction: Bringing Together Research and Practice

On my office bulletin board hangs an impassioned note from Heather, a former student. She explains why, in my geometry classroom, she disliked group work and preferred, overall, to work independently. She articulates what did not work for her about the cooperative learning structures I used as a beginning teacher. I have saved her note all these years for several reasons: First, it makes me smile. I am charmed by her earnest teenage passion, expressed in the capitalization of entire words (some of which are multiply underlined) and the sentences closed with profuse exclamation points. I am also glad that she trusted me enough to communicate her concerns. At the same time, Heather raises thoughtful questions that highlight the complexity of collaborative learning.

My favorite part of her note: *I understand that in the teaching world studies show how well kids do by doing group work, but that is on the <u>AVERAGE</u>. . . . My own study shows that I learn better in an environment that I prefer to be in not one I'm stuck in!!*

As Heather aptly observes, research must be squared with experience. Though something may be true "on the *average*," none of us lives in the world in general. We must contend the particularity that comes with human diversity. That complexity challenges our faith in that which only *tends* to be true.

I bring to the writing of this book an unusual set of experiences with collaborative learning. Over almost two decades as a classroom teacher, researcher, and teacher educator, I have come to understand group work in secondary mathematics classrooms. Adolescents are typically highly social creatures, and from the time I started teaching, harnessing their desire to interact toward the goal of academic learning seemed sensible. As a student teacher, I was interested in how different classroom arrangements could support students' participation and learning. I experimented with different configurations for collaborative learning, using everything from familiar small-group work lessons to more experimental learning-center structures that I adapted from elementary teaching methods.

My first full-time teaching position was in a diverse urban high school that brought together students from dozens of cultures. I had a strong sense that I could leverage my students' rich variety of languages and experiences by giving them opportunities to think through mathematics problems together. I worked largely on instinct, with a few principles about and tools for mathematics teaching to guide me.

My teaching experiments confirmed that, for mathematics to make sense, children's own thinking needed to be engaged. Daily, I saw students make important connections and arrive at deeper understandings. They needed to put ideas in their own words, understand why formulas or methods worked, and ask questions without a fear of looking dumb. These learning goals required sensitive attention to the social world of the classroom, because my activities would occasionally backfire. One such occasion prompted Heather's note. The bad days helped me learn, too; for instance, we needed a high degree of trust among us for students' emergent thinking to be safely aired. I tinkered with rules and routines and ultimately met with mostly positive but inconsistent success in my use of collaborative learning. Nonetheless, these experiences gave me a strong set of intuitions about students working together.

As I trained to become a researcher, I learned about a system for collaborative learning developed by Elizabeth Cohen called complex instruction (CI). Unlike most theories I encountered in graduate school, I did not first learn about CI from a book or article. I came across CI when I saw it put into practice by a team of dedicated teachers who had worked for more than a decade to figure out how it might support their project of detracking their urban high school's mathematics department.

I spent time watching these teachers' classes. As in my own urban high school classrooms, the students came from diverse cultural and linguistic backgrounds and were mostly working class. In several ways, though, the classes stood apart from the dozens of other mathematics lessons I had observed:

- Students were generally happy to be in math class.

- Teachers and students shared a warm connection.

- Students seemed comfortable with themselves and the content, tackling hard problems and discussing their ideas vigorously.

- Teachers posed challenging questions that, in my experience, would cause other classrooms to mutiny.

Students experienced this high level of content mostly positively. (See Horn [2006], just one example of my writing about teachers in this math department.) I think even Heather might have felt satisfied. When asked, more than the usual number reported that mathematics was their favorite subject. I was intrigued. As I was getting to know the school for a research project, I got the chance to teach a section of algebra alongside these teachers. Even though this approach was not typical for conducting research, I leapt at the chance. Thus, the second way I dove into CI was by using it in my own teaching, alongside experienced and generous colleagues.

Only as I wrote up my study did I read Elizabeth Cohen and Rachel Lotan's research to understand CI's theoretical and empirical grounding. I had not set out to study CI, but it happened to be a central pedagogy in the group of teachers I was working with. Since then, Rachel has generously helped me get a handle on CI research, guiding my understanding and answering my questions about the history of CI.

After getting to know CI myself, I faced the challenge of communicating it to teachers who did not have the same immersive introduction to it. In my work as a teacher educator, I have tried to merge the practical and theoretical traditions of CI, bringing to this endeavor expertise in research in mathematics education. I write this book from the perspective of a teacher educator, contributing a synthesis of mathematics education and CI research with the wisdom of expert practitioners. I articulate a subject-specific version of equitable collaborative learning that is deeply rooted in research and practice.

I hope that my experiences as a teacher educator add another layer to this work. As someone who works with both preservice and in-service mathematics teachers, I have come to know the conceptual challenges that collaborative learning poses. This work has given me insight into potential obstacles and some good strategies for pressing past them. As with my learning of the practical and theoretical side of CI, I have had good company in this venture. I have gleaned invaluable wisdom from other teacher educators who focus on bringing CI to secondary mathematics classrooms, particularly Carlos Cabana, Kristina Dance Peterson, Laura Evans, Lisa Jilk, Karen O'Connell, Barbara Shreve, Phil Tucher, and Ruth Tsu. I share some of their voices throughout the text.

Because my research focuses on teachers' learning of ambitious pedagogies (of which CI is one), I have studied teachers' learning of new practices in different teaching contexts. In this capacity, I have watched as teachers try to create this kind of equitable collaborative learning in their classrooms. With the help of research assistants Nicole Bannister, Sarah Sunshine Campbell, Audra Gray, Lauren Persky, and Maxine Alloway, I have interviewed teachers about what is most useful and challenging about implementing these methods. Watching and supporting teachers in different school settings has given me a better handle on some challenges that this learning brings up, both pedagogically and mathematically, thanks to insights from mathematicians Jim King and Ginger Warfield. I am grateful to these teachers for sharing their classrooms and their learning with me and to my collaborators for helping me think carefully about what we observed. Conversations with Laura Evans and Teresa Dunleavy helped me think more deeply about important issues. Generous and thoughtful commentary on earlier drafts of the manuscript came from Kara Jackson, Rachel Lotan, Ruth Tsu, Jim King, and Nicole Bannister. Their ideas helped sharpen my writing. Research and editorial assistance by Britnie Kane contributed strength and clarity to the manuscript. Lee Druce helped improve the graphic images. Further editorial support came from the excellent Gabe Waggoner at NCTM.

This book is my attempt to integrate the variety of experiences that contributed to my understanding of equitable collaborative learning in secondary mathematics classrooms. I hope that this book—arising from my background as a mathematics teacher, researcher, and teacher educator—serves as a useful guide for ambitious practitioners, school coaches, or other teacher educators. It introduces concepts and tools that are theoretically sound, empirically grounded, and practically useful for creating equitable collaborative learning environments in secondary mathematics classrooms.

My holding on to Heather's letter all these years is significant: she has become one of many student test cases that I use to think through any teaching strategy I encounter. As my story reveals, Heather, along with many others, has contributed to my understanding of the complex teaching practice I share with you here. I am grateful for the opportunity to have learned alongside such thoughtful people. I have no doubt that I am not as smart alone as I am together with them. Nonetheless, any errors that remain are my own.

Shifting Expectations:
Classrooms as Learning Environments

Vignette 1: Students Learning Together

The students in Ms. Shaw's ninth-grade class are working on the following probability problem:

> Imagine that you have two pockets and that each pocket contains a penny, a nickel, and a dime. You reach in and remove one coin from each pocket. Assume that for each pocket, the penny, the nickel, and the dime are equally likely to be removed. What is the probability that your two coins will total exactly two cents?

Steven, Antonio, Olivia, and Fasik sit together around a table. To determine the denominator of the probability, they have been counting all the possible coin combinations on their individual papers. They have been debating the number of possible outcomes.

Steven wrote the following:

(P, P) (P, N) (P, D) (N, D) (N, N) (D, D) (N, P) (D, P) (N, N)

9 possible

Antonio wrote this:

D __ P __ P   P __ D __ D   D __ N __ N

     | | |

     N   N   P

9 ways

    Steven and Antonio seem to agree that nine combinations of coins are possible. Then Antonio pauses and says, "But there are *two* pockets, so it's 18."

    "Why do you want to multiply?" asks Steven. Olivia laughs. Quietly, Fasik says he got six ways, because he counted (N, D) and (D, N) as the same outcome. Hearing the other students, though, he changes his response to nine.

What just happened would be a point of breakdown in many classrooms. Fasik and Antonio have miscounted the outcomes for different reasons. Their responses use some logic, but at this point making sense of each other's thinking is hard.

Key ideas of probability underlie this confusion:

- How do you count the coins systematically to find all the outcomes?

- How do you account for the two pockets in your counting?

- What counts as a unique outcome?

These are questions that need to be raised and then answered for this activity to be mathematically meaningful for the students. Fortunately, Ms. Shaw can draw on resources to move this conversation from the point of breakdown to a mathematically meaningful interaction.

Ms. Shaw, along with her colleagues, has worked on an approach to group work in her classroom designed to support learning by engaging students in thinking about such vital mathematical questions. Having students work together on rich problems allows them to bring up their mathematical understandings to serve as a foundation for their learning. Ms. Shaw and her colleagues use Elizabeth Cohen's (1994) seminal work on collaborative learning to support students in airing their thinking and guide them toward deeper understandings of mathematics.

By structuring an activity that raises these fundamental mathematical issues, Ms. Shaw has already done crucial work in engaging the students' sense making. As educators, we want to ensure that students will build on these preliminary understandings to come to mathematically sound ones.

Vignette 2: Facilitating Deeper Sense Making

Ms. Shaw is circulating around the classroom. This group is at an impasse. Kneeling on the floor to be at eye level with the students, she smiles and says, "You're arguing. I love arguing! Okay, Fasik. Tell me what the argument is about." The other students all start talking over Fasik. Ms. Shaw holds up her hand, signaling them to be quiet.

Fasik, a recent immigrant who is learning English, points to the (N, D) and (D, N) on his paper and says hesitatingly, "These two are the same." He also points to (P, N) and (N, P) along with (P, D) and (D, P), saying, "And these and these."

"Fancy set notation!" says Ms. Shaw. "Does everybody see what Fasik is thinking?"

Steven then speaks up, "No, they are different because they are in a different order."

Antonio loses his patience and says, "But I get 18 'cause you have two pockets, so it's all of this"—he circles his finger around his tree diagram—"times two."

Ms. Shaw turns to Olivia. "What do you think?" Olivia says she agrees with Steven "that it's just nine."

"Because?" Ms. Shaw asks, her eyebrows raised expectantly.

"Because those"—Olivia points to the (N, D) and (D, N) on Fasik's paper—"are different and the two pockets doesn't matter."

"Okay. Let's see," Ms. Shaw says. "How are we going to straighten this out? I like your diagram, Antonio. Let's see whether we can use it to answer this question." She puts Antonio's paper in the center of the table and then acts out the scenario. "Okay, you get a penny out of one pocket, right?" She pretends to pull a penny out of her pocket. "And out of the other pocket, you can get another penny. Where is that outcome on Antonio's diagram?"

Ms. Shaw continues to act out the outcomes, asking the students to find each event on Antonio's diagram.

Complicated pedagogical work happens in this second vignette. To support her students in airing their thinking, Ms. Shaw acknowledges the importance of mathematical disagreements ("I love arguing!"). At the same time, she evaluates the quality of their arguments, making it clear that students need to justify their positions ("Because?" she prompts Olivia later in the conversation). Second, she manages students' attention in important ways. She helps Fasik, hesitant to speak in front of his peers, to get the floor by signaling his groupmates to be quiet. She puts his paper in a place that his peers can see, allowing him to use simple language ("These two are the same") alongside his solution to explain his thinking about complex ideas. All the while, Ms. Shaw talks with this group and scans the rest of the classroom to make sure the other students are staying focused. She prioritizes quality conversations with her students and knows ahead of time what to monitor for and some key questions that will help her quickly assess any group's progress.

Although Antonio and Fasik's answers are wrong, she praises the systematic representations they have made in trying to solve this problem. These ways of counting are an important start toward an accurate answer, and Ms. Shaw realizes that the boys need a better idea of exactly what they are counting. Because Antonio is the only one to use the tree notation, she puts his work at the center during her enactment of the coin pulling. Doing so not only values the intellectual contribution of his work but also helps the other students understand an important representation for counting a sample space.

In this book, I will illuminate some of the concepts and tools that Ms. Shaw and her colleagues have used to shift their classrooms into places that support the development of students' mathematical thinking.

Developing Understanding in Different Learning Environments

How do we teach more students harder mathematics? American mathematics teachers are under pressure to increase the rigor of their courses while simultaneously making them accessible to more students. Unlike a mere twenty years ago, the upper-level mathematics curriculum is not solely the province of the college-bound. State and national standards, increased graduation requirements, and the expansion of standardized testing have raised the bar for all students, so teachers must bring challenging mathematics to a broader range of learners.

During that same period, we have discovered much more about how people learn mathematics. Studies of expert performance show that deep conceptual understanding of mathematics is needed to use that knowledge in different contexts. Consider that, in Ms. Shaw's classroom, the students have an opportunity to make sense of the idea of a *sample space*. In their daily lives, they will not have to worry about the two-pocket coin problem. But they will need a flexible conceptual understanding of probabilistic reasoning, because many financial and medical decisions require an understanding of these concepts. If students develop a good grasp of core ideas in Ms. Shaw's classroom, they are in a much better position to take charge of those consequential choices in their futures.

Teachers need to create *learning environments* that support student participation (Bransford, Brown, and Cocking 2000). Learning environments include the activities, context, roles, and relationships that participants have in a given setting that shape meanings and, consequentially, understandings. Thinking about the classroom as a learning environment means thinking not only about what the teacher is doing but also about the activities, the students, and the students' roles and relationships with one another, the teacher, and the content.

Ms. Shaw and her colleagues have chosen a rich problem that students can engage with. They use deliberate structures to involve students with the problem and monitor their progress. They no longer simply plan what they, as teachers, will do in the classroom. They have to develop a set of principles, structures, and strategies for interacting with students around mathematics. In this way, students have opportunities to engage their own ideas in various ways: drawing their own representations, discussing ideas with each other, justifying their ideas, and airing their confusions.

That last point is essential. When teachers provide a place for students' prior knowledge, children develop a more robust understanding of ideas. Too often in school, students learn what they need to know for a test and then revert to their misconceptions in their daily lives, failing to make critical connections between what they learned and how they live. Students lose learning between courses, leading teachers to complain of poor retention. The more varied ways of knowing, representing, and talking about math that are accepted, the greater the chances that more students will feel that their prior knowledge is valuable and that they will be able to make the meaningful connections that lead to understanding. Teachers need to respond to thinking that they may not always anticipate, increasing the complexity of the work.

For all this to be possible, students need to feel comfortable in their mathematics classrooms. Mathematics is notoriously disliked as a subject, the butt of jokes on TV shows and in comic strips. Particularly by adolescence, students have firm ideas about *who* is good at math—ideas often based on stereotypes of class, race, gender, or reputations of prior academic achievement. By valuing different mathematical contributions along with correct responses, such as Antonio's tree representation, Ms. Shaw and her colleagues redefine what being smart in math class means, giving more students an intellectually legitimate way into the subject. At the same time, by valuing the intellectually diverse mathematical contributions of their students, these teachers open the door for their own professional learning. The focus on student thinking requires a genuine curiosity about young people and their ideas.

> "Kids walk into math class thinking that school is about producing something on paper. I need to change their mind and get them to see it's about learning: starting with what they know, getting confused, and then developing tools to get through that confusion. The most important tools come from working with each other: listening, communicating, working through, and persisting. In the end I want it to be about 'Do I get this? Do you get that?' Writing it down is the last step."
>
> —*Laura Evans, Complex Instruction Educator, Mathematics Teacher, and Coach*

How Might Collaborative Learning Address Problems with Typical Math Instruction?

For several reasons, typical mathematics instruction has not succeeded for most learners. According to the Organization for Economic Cooperation and Development's PISA 2009 study, not only do American fifteen-year-olds underperform in mathematics compared with their age-mates in other countries, but also the negative impact of socioeconomic status on mathematical performance is greater here. Although enrollment in advanced mathematics classes has increased overall with changing graduation requirements, many poor students and students from historically disenfranchised ethnic and racial groups do not enroll in advanced mathematics (Planty, Provasnik, and Daniel 2007).

In secondary mathematics classrooms, the focus on teacher talk during instruction leaves students in the role of moving lessons forward by supplying answers to relatively simple questions:

> *Teacher:*   See the vertical angle here. It measures what?
>
> *Student:*   70?
>
> *Teacher:*   Right, 70 degrees.

This pattern of instructional dialogue is called *IRE*, which stands for initiation–response–evaluation (Cazden 2001). The teacher *initiates* an interaction by posing a question. Students then *respond* to the question. Then the teacher *evaluates* their answers.

According to the Third International Mathematics and Science Study (TIMSS), the dominant pattern of classroom instruction in the United States is *learning terms and practicing procedures*

(Stigler and Hiebert 1999). IRE discourse supports this form of mathematics instruction. Teachers give students definitions or demonstrate procedures. Then teachers question to see whether the students can recall the definition or apply the procedure to similar problems during instruction. Although the TIMSS study is more than a decade old, more recent studies of classroom teaching confirm that few mathematics lessons include opportunities for student sense making or questions that move understanding forward (Banilower et al. 2006). That is, the emphasis on deep conceptual understanding of mathematics needed for flexible thinking is missing.

IRE discourse is not inherently problematic. It has a role in many kinds of instructional conversations. Even in Ms. Shaw's classroom, we see moments of IRE structure in vignette 2, when she asks, "Where is that outcome on Antonio's diagram?"

However, student learning opportunities in her classroom are qualitatively different because of how the overall environment is organized. For instance, the students had a chance to make sense of the problem before she questioned them. In this way, the issues of uniqueness that come out in Fasik and Antonio's solutions are more authentic for the students than if she simply told the students how to ensure the correct sample space. Also, many questions she posed require more challenging mathematical thinking than they would in an IRE-dominated learning environment. For example, the students all produced different representations of the sample space. When Ms. Shaw organized the conversation around Antonio's tree diagram, the students had to make connections between their representation of the possible outcomes and his. They are also pressed to explain their thinking, not simply to produce a correct answer. In fact, if Ms. Shaw were looking only at their written work, she would not see Antonio's confusion about the two pockets or Fasik's about the distinction between (N, D) and (D, N) as outcomes.

Traditional IRE-dominated classrooms that focus on learning terms and practicing procedures constitute a kind of learning environment, even though they are not envisioned in this way. In these learning environments, quick, accurate recall and calculation are often the most important ways of being smart. If we look at the learning environment, this makes sense. Correct answers keep the lessons moving forward in an IRE dialogue, so they are valued, often at the expense of valuing students' mathematical thinking. In contrast, in our vignette, Antonio's incorrect answer of 18 outcomes in the sample space did not preclude Ms. Shaw from valuing his sophisticated tree representation.

Traditional learning environments give the impression that mathematics questions only ever require a short time to solve. Mathematician and educational researcher Alan Schoenfeld (1988) has documented this common belief among students and linked it to traditional instruction. Unlike the worksheets that include similar problems of increasing difficulty—a hallmark of traditional classrooms—the probability task presented here was one of three that Ms. Shaw's students were thinking about that day. By giving fewer problems that demand a greater depth of thinking, Ms. Shaw allowed her students opportunities to make important connections by giving sustained attention to their work.

> *By giving fewer problems that demand a greater depth of thinking, Ms. Shaw allowed her students opportunities to make important connections by giving sustained attention to their work.*

In a traditional setting, learners receive knowledge passively. Their individual understandings and identities do not influence what goes on in the classroom. In contrast, the students in our vignette are actively involved in making sense of the mathematics. Their confusions and disagreements become the basis for the instructional dialogue. With instruction focused on students' ideas, students not only feel intellectually valued but also have the potential to find a place for their out-of-school selves. Educational researchers Jo Boaler and James Greeno (2002) compared high school calculus classes that engaged students in mathematical ideas with more traditionally didactic classes. Students reported feeling like they "fit" more in the classrooms that incorporated dialogic classrooms than in the classrooms that relied heavily on the teacher's monologue. Students learn not just about mathematics in school but also about who they are as mathematics learners.

In addition to keeping students' sense of self outside the classroom doors, traditional mathematics classrooms make participation optional. Students know if they hang back and wait, another "smarter" student will supply the missing answer. Because classroom participation and achievement are related (Cohen 1994), a classroom where participation is optional disadvantages students who are reluctant to participate, whether due to their temperaments or their prior achievement. A collaborative learning environment strives to increase student learning by increasing participation. Mindful of this connection, Ms. Shaw drew Olivia and Fasik, who were both relatively quiet, into the conversation by soliciting their thinking.

Traditional mathematics instruction has not reached all students equitably. Although all students can be taught mathematics at a greater level of depth, historically marginalized groups of students are often severely underserved in mathematics classrooms. As we witnessed in Ms. Shaw's classroom, teachers can encourage recent immigrants like Fasik to speak in small-group settings. Group work also allows nonverbal representations of mathematics to play a larger role in the classroom. When students create and discuss their own representations, such as Antonio's tree diagram of the sample space, it not only highlights their sophisticated thinking but also might give English language learners, or others who might struggle with academic language, greater access to the mathematical content. In fact, small-group settings furnish important settings for English language learners to develop their facility with academic language (Gibbons 2003).

Summary

In this chapter, I outlined the motivation for finding new ways of organizing the learning environment of the classroom by comparing traditional instruction to the ideal implementation of collaborative classrooms. I held up an *ideal* collaborative classroom, because many attempts to incorporate collaborative learning often fall short of this. In this book, I outline a set of concepts and tools that can help teachers adjust their instruction to consider the whole learning environment of the classroom and to move their collaborative learning toward this ideal (see table 1.1).

In chapter 2, I will discuss more fully equitable classroom learning environments and how collaborative learning can contribute—or sometimes work against—student participation. In the chapters that follow, I introduce some concepts, strategies, and tools for supporting successful group work in the mathematics classroom.

The goal of this book is to support teachers in developing tools for effective group work in their secondary mathematics classrooms. Effective group work can leverage the learning potential of student-to-student interaction. It can also address some problems in typical mathematics instruction by supplying a framework for teachers to create engaging learning environments. Like all complex tools, group work needs to be used carefully to be effective. Thus, I will outline ways to choose tasks, help students adjust to new ways of approaching schooling, and address the kinds of status problems that can threaten the most earnest attempts at collaborative learning.

"One of the big shifts is moving away from being an 'I-teacher' to being a 'them-teacher.' Instead of asking yourself, 'What do *I* say now? What do *I* do next?' you ask, 'What do *they* need next? What are *they* doing?'"

—*Laura Evans, Complex Instruction Educator, Mathematics Teacher, and Coach*

Table 1.1. Shifts in major components of the teaching system moving from a traditional to a collaborative learning environment

Component	Learning Environment	
	Traditional	**Collaborative**
Teacher role	• Effective presentation of ideas • Attending to correct answers	• Designing effective learning environments • Instruction centered on student thinking
Mathematics	• Ready-made: nothing to figure out, just to receive • Hierarchical view: sequential topics organized so that one cannot progress without mastering prerequisites	• In the making: students can make sense of mathematics • Connected view: a network of ideas whose connections students can explore through different forms of mathematical thinking
How to be smart in mathematics	• Quick, accurate recall and calculation • Complete worksheets with many problems of increasing difficulty	• Create sophisticated visual and symbolic representations of mathematical thinking • With peers, analyze fewer problems that require a greater depth of thinking
Pace of mathematics classes	• Mathematics problems take a short time to solve	• Mathematics problems must be considered in depth to be understood
Student role	• Students are passive recipients of knowledge • Individual understandings and identities do not influence the classroom • Work completion most highly valued form of participation	• Students' confusion and disagreements are expected and become the basis for instructional dialogue • Students have the potential to find a place for their broader identities • Careful thinking most highly valued form of participation
Participation demands	• Participation is optional • Wait for the "smart" student to answer questions • Status strongly influences participation	• Participation is expected of every student, regardless of prior achievement or temperament • Increase participation by fostering equal-status interactions
Assessment tools	• Contribute to comparison and competition among students • Make definitive judgments about achievement and smartness	• Focus on individuals' learning • Encourage persistence by offering opportunities to revise
Multiyear learning	• Prioritizes teacher autonomy • Little to no coordination across mathematics classrooms	• Prioritizes student learning • Careful sequencing of mathematics and student skills to assist in the development of both

Equitable Mathematics Teaching

In the last chapter, I touched on a fundamental dilemma that mathematics teachers face. How do we teach mathematics to make it rigorous and accessible? Ms. Shaw's classroom showed how strategic use of collaborative learning afforded both rigor and access, as students with various mathematical, cultural, and linguistic backgrounds worked together to make sense of important mathematical ideas.

To implement this kind of group work, one must understand how Ms. Shaw's teaching fits in the broader landscape of *equitable mathematics teaching:* modes of instruction that optimally support meaningful mathematical learning for all students.

> *Equitable mathematics teaching involves using modes of instruction that optimally support meaningful mathematical learning for all students.*

To teach mathematics meaningfully, I envision students who do not simply know math facts but are mathematically literate. They can apply their mathematical knowledge as students, workers, citizens, and critical consumers of the quantitative information underlying consequential decisions in their lives. Mathematically literate people fluently use mathematics. It is a meaningful way for them to engage with and interpret the world.

I build the following framework for equitable mathematics teaching from more than two decades of educational research that has sought to understand how to simultaneously give students access mathematics while maintaining rigor. This research, along with related experiences working with teachers and students in schools, is the focus of this chapter.

Principles for Collaborative Learning Environments

Although the scope of this book does not allow for a complete review of research on equitable mathematics teaching, the literature does show that progress toward equitable mathematics teaching requires work within and beyond individual classrooms. In reviewing this work on equitable mathematics teaching, I found three main levels of teaching practices that increased access to meaningful mathematics for all students: school, department, and classroom. The kinds of teaching practices reported to influence equitable mathematics teaching could be sorted into three categories:

1. *What counts as math* involves how mathematics is presented to students and the messages about what success means.

2. *Pedagogical practices* focus on the work of teaching.

3. *Relational practices* address the relationships that students build with others in the school and classroom.

I present an overview of this research in table 2.1 and in the following narrative. This table signals the multiple levels at which issues of equitable mathematics teaching need to be addressed. In this chapter, I will summarize the findings of this body of research and use it to articulate a set of principles that guide the implementation of these practices in the classrooms where I have worked. I will use chapters 3–8 to relate these principles to specific teaching practices.

I will review the research summarized in table 2.1 by going down the columns. I focused on studies that demonstrated ways to move students deeper into mathematical thinking, as well as those that contributed to our understanding of equitable learning environments, particularly in secondary mathematics. Relationships exist both across the rows and down the columns, but I narrate this way to emphasize the multiple levels of organization at which these different goals work to support equitable mathematics learning.

What Counts as Mathematics

In the conception of equity I propose, equitable mathematics teaching supports meaningful mathematical learning for all students. Mathematics cannot be meaningful if the subject itself has not been represented richly. Doing so requires deliberate efforts from the school, department, and classroom. On the largest scale described here, schools furnish teachers with well-articulated and rigorous mathematics curriculum (Stigler and Hiebert 1999; Boaler 2002). They support teachers' effective use of curriculum by hiring quality teachers who are knowledgeable about students and content (Hill, Rowan, and Loewenberg 2005) and then support the teachers by offering ongoing professional development (Schoenfeld 2002). If needed, students should get positive support outside instruction to help them with their academic skills (Treisman 1992).

At the department level, teachers work together to constantly deepen their ideas about mathematics (Moses and Cobb 2001). The teachers ensure the quality of the curriculum by focusing it on important mathematical ideas (Boaler 2002). Working together, teachers can decide what is important to teach (Boaler 2002). They build lessons around activities that develop students' procedural fluency, conceptual understanding, and problem-solving skills (Schoenfeld 2002). As teachers lead students through the curriculum, multiyear alignment seems necessary for closing achievement disparities among student groups (Boaler 2002). Although teaching practice is typically conceived as what happens within classrooms, what happens across classrooms appears to be highly consequential. In equitable settings, judgments about promotion make clear distinctions between students' abilities to do school (doing homework, staying organized) and their abilities to do mathematics (Horn 2006). A student who fails to turn in work but has demonstrated a strong understanding of the content, for instance, would not automatically be retained. For part of those decisions, teachers use high-quality assessments that focus on student learning and capture the richness of the mathematics being taught and minimize bias against students because of language, class, or cultural backgrounds (Schoenfeld 2002).

Within their classrooms, individual teachers build learning environments that build on students' prior knowledge (Moll et al. 1992). They value multiple approaches to mathematical ideas (Boaler 2002), focusing on connections and meaning (Kazemi 1998). Classes offer opportunities to engage deeply in the content, with teachers modeling high-level performances and pressing students for justification (Boaler 2002; Kazemi 1998). At the same time, students receive appropriate scaffolds that do not take away from the quality of the mathematics by turning rich problems into rote procedure (Stein et al. 2008). As teachers listen to students, they take many kinds of

Table 2.1. Synthesis of the literature on equitable mathematics teaching practices

Level	What Counts as Mathematics	Pedagogical Practices	Relational Practices
School/ department	• Well-articulated, rigorous curriculum • Knowledgeable teaching staff • Ongoing professional development • Nonstigmatized supplemental support for student learning	• Collective responsibility for student success • Sharing of teaching resources • Coordinated expectations for behavior and learning across classrooms • Norms balancing coordination and professional discretion in making teaching decisions	• Culture of caring for students • Supports for creating identities of achievement • Recognition of community educational values
Department or individual classroom	• Rethinking assumptions about subject matter • Curriculum focused on important mathematical ideas • Emphasize depth over coverage • Distinguish between doing math and doing school • Emphasize problem solving and skill development • High-quality assessment aligned with curricular goals	• Clear expectations for behavior and learning • Enough time for students to work with complex ideas • Emphasize the role of effort in learning • Innovating to respond to students	• Support for navigating peer, home, and school worlds • Noncompetitive learning environments • Focus on students' mathematical dispositions
Classroom	• Building on students' prior knowledge • Valuation of multiple approaches to mathematical ideas • Focus on connections and meaning • High press for justification • High-level performance modeled • Appropriate scaffolds • Attention to representation and gesture in the construction of mathematical meaning	• Focus on student learning in teaching and assessments • Explicit teaching of learning practices • Appropriate amount of time • Engagement with partial or tentative responses • Normalization of mistakes as a part of learning	• Building relationships with students • Attention to affective dimensions of learning (e.g., math phobia, belonging) • Attention to students' interactions with each other (relational equity) • Belief in students' competence

contributions beyond correct answers. Students can build meaning through questions, gesture, and representations of mathematical ideas (Moschkovich 1999). Their performances are judged on assessments that focus on learning (Black et al. 2004).

Pedagogical Practices

If equitable mathematics teaching involves using modes of instruction that optimally support meaningful mathematical learning for all students, pedagogical practices require consideration at multiple levels of organization. At the school level, all personnel in the building, from administrators to counselors to teachers, need to invest themselves in students' success (Lee and Smith 1996; Gutierrez 1996). To this end, teaching resources should be shared. Schoolwide expectations for behavior and learning can minimize difficulties that arise from transitions across teachers and classes (Horn 2008b). Imagining developing such broad consensus about teaching, many teachers cringe. Coordination of teaching practices, however, does not preclude some professional discretion in making teaching decisions (Horn 2006).

At the department level, teachers can collectively set clear expectations for behavior and learning within their subject area. Significantly, departments that have shown to narrow or close disparities in student achievement work across multiple years. Equity cannot be achieved in one year because it depends on students' ultimate achievement level across the curriculum (Horn 2004). As they articulate their courses, teachers must give students enough time to work with complex ideas across grade levels (Henningsen and Stein 2002). Policies about promotion and retention should be organized for advancement (Gutierrez 1996), circumventing bureaucracy in the interest of helping students progress through the curriculum. For example, if a student meets the requirements to go up a level in mathematics midyear, teachers can work together to help that student do so. Such structure emphasizes the role of effort in learning and deemphasizes prior achievement, which may be limited owing to lack of opportunity (Stodolsky and Grossman 2000). It also shows innovation on the part of teachers that serves students' needs (McLaughlin and Talbert 2001).

Classroom teaching focuses on student learning over behavior management (Horn 2006). Positive behavior comes from students' engagement in the subject matter. Teachers give students opportunities to access content by teaching them explicitly how to learn in their classroom (Boaler 2002). If these routines and structures are held constant at the department level, students' opportunities for success increase over their years in school. Just as at the department level, curriculum should be paced to give students the right amount of time to engage in ideas deeply while pushing to prepare them for college (Henningsen and Stein 2002). Earlier I stressed the need for broader acceptance of student contributions to signal a richer conception of mathematics (Gresalfi et al. 2009). Likewise, when teachers build off a wider range of contributions, including questions, mistakes, gestures, and representations, they in turn value the participation of a wider range of students. To this end, teachers should consider mistakes a normal part of sense making (Stigler and Hiebert 1999).

Relational Practices

Supporting the mathematical learning of all students means supporting the participation of all students. Students who tend not to participate often report feeling alienated from school in general or mathematics classes in particular. A set of relational practices can contribute to equitable mathematics teaching by giving students a sense of belonging and offer an inroad to their mathematical engagement and learning.

Schools with a culture of caring are unmistakable. A visitor steps in, and students show an eagerness to welcome the newcomer. They may offer directions or just a smile; the divide between adults and adolescents that exists at some schools is not present. Instead, students have ownership and pride in their learning that they are eager to share. When these schools' sense of caring is coupled with high expectations, the effect on students is powerful (Nieto and Bode 2011). Perhaps it is through the displays of student work that line the walls. Perhaps it is the sense of purpose that one feels as students transition from class to class, with minimal hallway loitering. No matter the details, caring schools clearly support students' identities as learners (Martin 2000). School leaders can profoundly influence a school culture, and the schools I have visited that have achieved this level of caring and purpose invariably have strong administrators at the helm (Bryk et al. 2010). The administrators work hard to communicate with parents and other educational stakeholders in the community to align their visions of success (Delpit 1995).

At the department level, teachers work together to help students navigate transitions between their peer, home, and school worlds (Phelan, Davidson, and Yu 1997). Teachers recognize that their students' linguistic and cultural backgrounds may differ from their own and pool their experiences to best respond to, build from, and respect these differences. These teachers create noncompetitive learning environments across classrooms to reinforce the emphasis on learning (Kelly and Turner 2009). They help students build positive mathematical dispositions, affirming that students have a place in a mathematical community, within and beyond individual classrooms (Gresalfi 2009).

Individual teachers build relationships to let their students know that they are valued members of the community (Nieto and Bode 2011). Not only are students valued as people, but they also have something to contribute intellectually (Allexsaht-Snider and Hart 2001). In classrooms, teachers attend to students' affective experience of mathematics, concerning themselves with the residue of negative past experiences and working to build a safe and caring environment (Cobb and Hodge 2002). Conversely, students' enthusiasm for the subject is embraced and not viewed negatively. To achieve this goal, teachers attend closely to classroom language and interaction to monitor negative talk about students' abilities. The result is a form of *relational equity* (Boaler and Staples 2008), a sense that all students have something valuable to contribute to the mathematical conversation. Underlying these efforts is a genuine belief in students' ability to improve their mathematical understanding, no matter what level they start from in their classrooms (Oakes et al. 2002).

You may notice that this literature review focuses on school-, department-, and classroom-level issues. These are within immediate reach of educators seeking to improve their schools' mathematics teaching and learning. Of course, larger sources of inequity exist in our society. To truly achieve equitable mathematics learning, schools should be equally resourced, students should have adequate nourishment and shelter, and the structural inequities that limit people's life choices would be mitigated (Martin 2006).

Principles for Equitable Mathematics Teaching

How do educators take this vision of equitable mathematical, pedagogical, and relational practices and translate it to their practice in the settings they control? In this section, I propose four principles for equitable mathematics teaching that capture the essence of these findings.

Principle 1: Learning Is Not the Same as Achievement

Students' mathematical competence is often conflated with their level of achievement, which is typically signaled by the math class that they are in. Teachers might vie for an honors class. Parents may fret when a student is held back. Both responses to students' achievement levels may be understandable, but neither achievement nor class level wholly reflects students' levels of ability or learning.

Although learning and achievement are related, they are not the same. Learning happens when students deepen and extend their knowledge of mathematical ideas. Achievement reflects how they are progressing in school. Most educators recognize the imperfect correlation: some students progress without understanding, whereas other students understand without progressing.

Low-achieving students often garner the most attention and concern in the home, in the school, and on the policy landscape. However, if we really commit to the notion that learning and achievement are not the same, we see that low-achieving students are not the only ones not learning mathematics deeply enough. Internationally, American students underperform in mathematics, especially in the secondary grades. According to the Organization for Economic Cooperation and Development's PISA 2009 study, not only do American fifteen-year-olds underperform in mathematics compared with their peers in other countries, but the negative impact of socioeconomic status on mathematical performance is also greater in the United States. All our students, regardless of achievement level, could be learning mathematics better. The issue of better mathematics education matters for students across the achievement spectrum. We need to do a better job teaching mathematics to everyone.

Principle 2: Achievement Gaps Often Reflect Gaps in Opportunities to Learn

Nonetheless, concerning demographic trends are evident in student achievement patterns. Although enrollment in advanced mathematics classes has increased overall because of changing graduation requirements, many poor students and students from historically disenfranchised racial and ethnic groups continue to opt out of advanced mathematics. Civil rights leader and mathematics educator Robert Moses compares the absence of math literacy in urban and rural communities throughout this country to an issue as urgent as the lack of black voters in Mississippi in 1960 (Moses and Cobb 2001).

Moses and others have productively recast the so-called *achievement gaps* as *opportunity gaps* (Moses and Cobb 2001). Different educational outcomes manifest themselves as disparate levels of achievement on standardized tests, but this focus on individual student achievement erases the radically different opportunities for mathematical learning that exist within and across our schools. Thinking about opportunity gaps raises a different set of issues for schools and teachers. Instead of the blame game that begins when we view our students as low-achieving (i.e., "if only their parents better supervised their homework"; "if only their prior teachers held them to higher standards"), we can think about how to re-create our classrooms and departments in ways that will increase the opportunities for students across achievement levels to learn by thinking mathematically.

> "Make the process of learning transparent to students. Tell them they should *expect* to get confused. Tell them in real time when a behavior they choose builds their understanding and even point out the opposite. Make learning a hike through peaks and valleys. It's the journey that builds understanding, not the destination."
> —*Laura Evans, Complex Instruction Educator, Mathematics Teacher, and Coach*

Principle 3: All Students Can Be Pushed to Learn Mathematics More Deeply

Opportunity gaps exist for students across the achievement spectrum. Although the social and economic consequences are greatest for low-achieving students, opportunity gaps affect all students. Middle-achieving students may simply get by in mathematics class without learning much, missing the chance to develop their own intellectual powers and foreclosing future educational opportunities. We all meet adults who regretfully confess having shaped their career paths around avoiding mathematics. Even high-achieving students need a better mathematics education. In our constant conflation of achievement level and learning, we often hurry students through the curriculum. As a result, high-achieving students might be pushed past the rich connections that engage them in the subject or offer some of the affective pleasure that might spur them on to study it at higher levels.

A key characteristic of equitable classrooms is that all students are supported to substantially participate in each phase of instruction, although not necessarily in the same ways. In equitable classrooms, all students should have opportunities to learn meaningful mathematics, no matter their prior achievement. Logically, then, teachers need to organize their classrooms into places where learning is the primary focus. Too often, mathematics classrooms hold as their goal work completion: a student is done when an assignment is finished. However, students not only need to finish assignments, they also need to be able to authentically engage with mathematical ideas with sustained attention. To do that, nearly all students need to be retaught how to learn mathematics. Some students are great learners outside the classroom but have not figured out how to be students yet. Their homework remains at the bottom of their backpack, if it is completed at all. They work in fits and starts, not recognizing that the reward system of school requires ongoing effort. Some students are great at school but manage to achieve without really understanding the material they have covered with any depth. They know how to keep an organized notebook, turn in homework, and study for tests, but their minds are not fully engaged in what they are doing. In the framework for equitable mathematics teaching, students need access to the tools to learn, no matter their prior achievement or competence as students.

For students who have not succeeded in school, this process often requires instruction in how to be a student. Student skills are teachable and may help us bring more children to mathematical success. Mathematics educator and researcher Jo Boaler calls these skills *learning practices* (Boaler 2002); students must be taught how to learn math. For example, students' gaps in their math facts may not be as big of a hurdle in teaching them algebra as their misunderstanding about what turning in daily homework means. We have all had students who turn in a wad of homework the week before a marking period ends with the idea of "making up points," unaware of the need to regularly turn homework in for both practice and credit.

We also need to teach students to learn and make sense of the work they are doing. Some students may be good at completing their work, but they do not yet know how to think carefully about the mathematics they are doing. Assignments are not simply about filling out a piece of paper with correct answers; they need to be an opportunity for sense making. We need to work with students to make our classrooms places where they complete mathematically meaningful work. I discuss this in more detail in chapter 4.

When mathematical knowledge is simply received through learning terms and practicing procedures, the subject becomes a set of arbitrary, disconnected rituals. Students learn content for tests and then promptly forget it. This way of presenting mathematics alienates students, making them less inclined to engage in learning the content. Such an approach takes away a key resource for persistence through tough problems and commitment to working through difficult ideas.

Another important resource that traditional teaching obscures is that mathematics *has logic* and *makes sense*. A simple example: a student with solid understanding of inverses and multiplication will deduce the need for division. Everything we learn to do in mathematics, we seek ways to undo, so it follows logically that the existence of multiplication will require an operation like division. When students understand the relationship between mathematical ideas and have developed what have been referred to as mathematical habits of mind (Cuoco, Goldenberg, and Mark 1996), the next topic for discussion often generates itself.

Principle 4: Students Need to See Themselves in Mathematics

Mathematics, as a subject, has a reputation for being interesting to a narrow group of people. In one study, young people were asked to draw a mathematician. Most drew unflattering pictures of scruffy men with pens in their pockets, holes in their clothes, and equations on their arms (MacLeod 2001): not exactly people children wish to emulate. In general, children do not see themselves as mathematicians in the same way they might see themselves as readers or artists. Consequently, adolescents' emergent identities typically do not adhere to mathematics in the same way they might to expressive subjects such as English or art.

The problem of alienation from mathematics is often exacerbated for students whose home culture or language differs from school culture. Even something as simple as the way that a question is phrased or singling out a student for praise may go against the grain of that student's home culture. When students do not see themselves in what they are learning, finding meaning in school activities is harder.

Related to the disaffection that comes from abandoning their sense of self, students often feel that mathematics allows no room for questioning. They perceive that ancient people figured out mathematics, which offers no inroads for their curiosity. Jo Boaler and James Greeno (2000) attribute this perception to how teachers often present mathematical knowledge in school, giving students little opportunity to engage their own ideas or to do their own sense making. In didactic teaching situations, students feel that their job is to receive preexisting knowledge. Students in these contexts commonly report disliking math, whereas students who learn mathematics in discussion-based classrooms see connections between the subject and their lives. They also report liking mathematics more. The researchers argue that the way we learn and our affective experience of the content are connected. The more room students have to engage them*selves* in their learning, the more fully they will be engaged.

Finally, we need to make our classrooms places that value not only the cultural and linguistic diversity of our students but also the intellectual diversity. Intellectual diversity, when nurtured, contributes to learning. As students consider other conceptions of the same idea and reconcile apparent differences, their understanding deepens. Yet most classrooms are organized so that only two kinds of mathematical smartness are valued: quickness and accuracy. Although quick and accurate calculations are often a benefit of a solid mathematics education, they are not the only measure of mathematical competence. Mathematics as a field owes its development to other kinds of smartness as well, including connecting two seemingly disparate ideas, posing a meaningful problem, or devising a useful representation. I will extend this critical discussion of smartness in chapter 3.

When I read applications for graduate school, I inevitably receive some essays from teachers who have noted the prevalence of math anxiety in their classrooms. This fourth principle is really about making a classroom learning environment where students feel ownership of their learning. It is a more productive way to think about math anxiety. The difference is crucial, though. *Anxiety* focuses on an individual's emotional experience, which perhaps cannot be helped. It gives you little to do as a teacher, other than reassure students or try to help them relax. If, instead, we focus on creating a classroom environment that fosters a sense of belonging and normalizes confusion, we, as teachers, have something to do.

Summary

The four principles presented in the framework for equitable teaching are foundational to this book's concepts and tools. Let's review the principles for equitable teaching and articulate how they focus on the relationship between students and mathematics.

Principle 1: Learning is not the same as achievement. By recognizing the distinction between learning and achievement, we open our eyes to the possibility that all students might have something mathematically important to contribute to our classrooms.

Principle 2: Achievement gaps often reflect gaps in opportunities to learn. Relatedly, by focusing on opportunity gaps rather than achievement gaps, we recognize that a history of low achievement may be more reflective of the different opportunities students have had in their education than of any innate ability.

Principle 3: All students can be pushed to learn mathematics more deeply. Just as changing our conception of low-achieving students is important, so it is with middle- and high-achieving students. Because I make important distinctions between achievement and learning, I recognize that even "successful" students may have significant gaps in their learning and need to be taught to think mathematically. Chapter 3 takes up this issue of mathematical smartness in more depth.

Principle 4: Students need to see themselves in mathematics. Finally, the framework recognizes that students come in with not only culturally and linguistically diverse backgrounds but also intellectually diverse ones. Equitable mathematics classrooms need to recognize and value this diversity by supplying mathematically rich activities for students to engage with meaningfully. Chapter 4 introduces groupworthy tasks, which you can use to ensure that students have access to meaningful mathematics.

Schwab's instructional triangle is often used to present the work of teaching, highlighting the relationships among key elements of instruction as in figure 2.1. As we consider the role of different teaching principles and practices, we can locate them on this diagram. The four principles presented in the framework for equitable mathematics teaching emphasize the connection between students and mathematics (fig. 2.2).

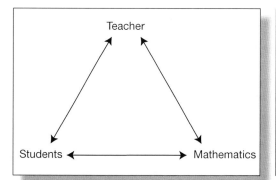

Fig. 2.1. The Schwabian triangle representing the key relationships in instruction

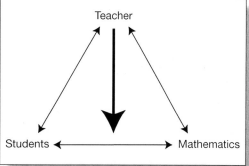

Fig. 2.2. The expanded instructional triangle (other researchers have used the instructional triangle as a motif for describing instruction, most extensively Magdalene Lampert [2003])

These principles are intended to help teachers reconceptualize the nature of that relationship as they rework their practice. We will revisit figure 2.2 throughout this text.

Mathematical Competence and Status: What "Being Smart" Means

In chapter 2, I laid out the following principles for equitable mathematics teaching, which should undergird collaborative learning in mathematics classrooms:

- Principle 1: Learning is not the same as achievement.

- Principle 2: Achievement gaps often represent gaps in opportunities to learn.

- Principle 3: All students can be pushed to learn mathematics more deeply.

- Principle 4: Students need to see themselves in mathematics.

Each principle influences the main topics of this chapter: mathematical competence and status. Mathematical competence has to do with a student's ability to complete a variety of mathematical tasks: his or her "smartness." Students can use and show their smartness through the structure of group work in many ways. A student's mathematical competence will often have direct bearing on his or her status in the classroom. Status is how competent a student both feels and is perceived to be by his or her classroom peers. Both concepts are important for students' learning and achievement, and both have important consequences for how successfully students will be able to carry out group work. Thus, understanding status and mathematical competence is foundational work for any teacher hoping to bring collaboration into the classroom.

The Organization of Smartness

By the time they are in secondary school, students enter their mathematics classes with strong ideas about who they and their peers are as mathematics learners. They can tell you who is smart and who is not. They base these judgments on earlier school achievement, as well as on categories such as race, class, popularity, and gender. These assessments play out in the classroom. Some students' contributions are sought out and heard, whereas others' contributions are ignored. This imbalance obstructs productive mathematical conversations because an argument's valuation comes from *who* is speaking and not *what* is being said.

This chapter addresses how to support productive mathematical conversations in the classroom by looking at important social dynamics. I will use the following definition:

> *Productive mathematical conversations are ones in which arguments are weighed on the basis of the mathematical validity of what is being said, not on who is speaking.*

Judgments about who is smart based on prior achievement or social categories violate a fundamental principle of equity and are consequential: *learning is not the same as achievement*. Confounding this problem, American schools tend to be organized in ways that obscure distinctions between learning and achievement. In fact, they are often built around the idea that differences in student achievement are the natural consequence of differences in ability. The logic of tracking, particularly in the early grades, rests on notions of identifiable differences in ability that require different approaches in teaching.

In reality, tracking often only reinforces achievement differences by giving high-achieving students better teaching and more enriched learning environments (Oakes 2005). Recall the second principle of equitable teaching discussed in chapter 2: *achievement gaps often reflect opportunity gaps*. We typically think of opportunity gaps as existing across schools, with schools serving upper middle-class populations having greater resources than schools serving poor students. Although this tragically remains the case in the United States (Kozol 1991), the resource differences within schools are often overlooked. Two students in the same school placed in different tracks—on the basis of their prior achievement—typically have radically different learning opportunities through the quality of their teachers, the time spent engaged in academic activities, and the rigor of the curriculum. Once you are behind, getting ahead is hard (Oakes 2005).

As chapter 2 noted, all students in the United States should have the opportunity to learn mathematics more deeply. In 2009, on an international measure sponsored by the Organization for Economic Cooperation and Development (OECD), fifteen-year-olds in the United States scored statistically significantly below the average, in comparison with other nations in the OECD, in mathematics. Indeed, among the OECD's thirty-four participating countries, the United States ranks twenty-fifth in mathematics achievement.

However, looking more closely at the data, one sees that although all students could benefit from higher-quality mathematics instruction, not all students are receiving equitable education. One can often predict these opportunity gaps by a student's race or socioeconomic status. In U.S. reading, mathematics, and science instruction, student socioeconomic status accounts for 17 percent of the variation in student performance. In higher-performing countries, such as Canada and Japan, socioeconomic status accounts for only 9 percent of the variation in student performance (OECD 2011).

The belief in ability as the root of different levels of achievement is so entrenched in the organization of curriculum and schooling that many people have a hard time imagining another model. Other conceptualizations are possible, however. Japanese education attributes differences in achievement to students' different levels of effort instead of differences in ability (Stevenson 1994). Classrooms are organized to see student differences as a resource for teaching, instead of viewing them as an obstacle to be accommodated. Tracking does not occur in the early grades.

Psychologists James Stigler and James Hiebert reported this distinction in data from the TIMSS video study, where they compared mathematics teaching in the United States, Germany, and Japan. They summarize some fundamental cultural beliefs that organize teaching, describing the Japanese view of student difference: "Individual differences are beneficial for the class because they produce a range of ideas and solution methods that provides the material for students' discussion and reflection. The variety of alternative methods allows students to compare them and construct connections among them. It is believed that all students benefit from the variety of ideas generated by their peers. In addition, tailoring instruction to specific students is seen as unfairly limiting and as prejudging what students are capable of learning: All students should have the opportunity to learn the same material" (Stigler and Hiebert 1999, p. 4).

Considering students' robust views on who is smart along with schooling practices such as tracking, which naturalize differences, it is no wonder that most students' mathematical self-concepts seem immutable by the time they arrive in secondary classrooms. Everything around them fixes their sense of their ability, be it low, high, or average.

Status versus Ability: Interrupting Ideas about Smartness

If learning is not the same as achievement, and if achievement gaps often reflect opportunity gaps, what do we make of students' prior achievement when they enter our classrooms? Who are the students who have succeeded in mathematics before entering our classrooms? How about those who have not? Disentangling achievement and ability may sound reasonable, but we need a new model for thinking about students we teach. Elizabeth Cohen's (1994) work on complex instruction frames these issues around *status,* a concept that clarifies the conflation of achievement and ability. *Status* gives teachers room to analyze this problem and respond through their instruction.

In this context, we will use the following definition of status:

> *Status is the perception of students' academic capability and social desirability.*

The word *perception* is key to this definition. Perception drives the wedge between social realities and perhaps yet unrealized possibilities of what students can do mathematically. Perception involves our expectations of what people have to offer.

Where do these status perceptions come from? As the chapter opener discusses, the perception of academic capability often comes from students' earlier academic performance. It might come from their academic track, with *honors* students having higher status than that of *regular* students. Status judgments about ability might also draw on stereotypes based on class, race, ethnicity, language, or gender.

The perception of social desirability arises from students' experiences with peers. For instance, students often see attractive peers as desirable friends—or perhaps just undesirable enemies. Likewise, whatever drives popularity in local teen culture will show up in the classroom as status. The team captain, the talented artist, or the cut-up rebel—whomever students clamor to befriend or win the approval of—will have higher social status.

> "Thinking about status issues is what, for me, differentiates complex instruction from just 'regular' group work. Addressing and being aware of status issues is what makes all the other interactions productively possible."
> —*Clint Chan, Mathematics Teacher*

Status plays out in classroom interactions. Students with high status have their ideas heard, have their questions answered, and are endowed with the social latitude to dominate a discussion. On the other side, students with low status often have their ideas ignored, have their questions disregarded, and often fall into patterns of nonparticipation or, worse, marginalization.

Recognizing the relationship between status and speaking rights highlights an important way for educators to uncover these issues in their classrooms. Status manifests through participation patterns. Who speaks, who stays silent, who is excluded, and who dominates class discussions are all indicators of status. Individually, this concept influences students' learning. If some students' ideas are continually ignored, their questions will go unanswered and their confusions will remain unaired. Over time, this system may reinforce negative ideas they have about themselves as mathematics learners, because they may conclude that their ideas are not valuable. Conversely, students whose ideas are consistently heard and worked with will have greater opportunities to engage and sort through them. Socially, if students' dominance becomes unregulated, they may develop an overblown sense of their value in the social and intellectual world of the classroom. Thus, status-driven interactions not only influence learning but also reinforce existing status hierarchies.

Skeptics might protest linking participation and status. "Some students are just shy," someone might say. That is true. Likewise, students learning English often go through a silent period or may be self-conscious of their accents. Our goal with reluctant speakers is to design ways for them to comfortably participate more than they are perhaps naturally inclined to do. As we will cover in chapter 5, strategies such as small-group talk first or individual think time may help build the confidence of shy or nervous speakers. The emphasis on participation in classroom discussions comes from several research studies showing that such involvement is essential to developing conceptual understanding and academic language (Cohen et al. 2002; Webb 1991).

Socially, status plays out in participation patterns. Individually, status influences students' mathematical self-concepts, or their ideas about what kind of math learners they are. As mathematics educators, we have all encountered students who claim that they are not "good at mathematics" before they even give a new idea a chance. Intuitively, we know that students' mathematical self-concept influences their motivation and effort in mathematical learning. If students *know* they are not good at mathematics, why should they push past their confusion when problems become difficult? If students *know* they are smart, why should they bother to explain their thinking, let alone pay attention to a classmate's? Students' self-concept is deeply tied to their attitudes about learning mathematics, in and out of our classrooms. Societal biases predispose students to think of themselves and their peers as more or less competent in mathematics, playing into students' choices to engage, persist, and take risks in the classroom.

> "My students and I talk a lot about what it looks like to be a powerful math learner—taking risks, contributing productively, and persisting. I've started making those behaviors transparent to students when they happen. We talk about how brains learn and how they should expect to move from surface knowledge to confusion to deeper understanding. I want them to experience that journey whenever I ask them to do tough math together (group work). I know group work is working when they take risks, contribute, and persist. It bleeds into whole-class discussions, too."
>
> —*Laura Evans, Complex Instruction Educator, Mathematics Teacher, and Coach*

Seeing Status in the Classroom

Status hierarchies manifest in classroom conversations and participation patterns, often leading to *status problems,* or the breakdown of mathematical communication based on status rather than the substance of mathematical thinking. Before we talk about remediating status problems, let's delineate how teachers can see status problems in their classrooms.

Participation

One of the most important and tangible status assessments teachers can do is ask who speaks and who is silent. Some students might dominate a conversation, never soliciting or listening to others' ideas. These are probably high-status students. Some students may make bids to speak that get steamrolled or ignored. Some students may seem to simply disappear when a classroom conversation gains momentum. These are probably low-status students.

If you want to get a better handle on the participation patterns in your classroom, give a colleague a copy of your seating chart and have this person sit in your classroom. He or she can check off who speaks during a class session. This simple counting of speaking turns (without worrying about content or length for the moment) can give you a sense of dominance and silence. Surprisingly, teachers' impressions of speaking turns are sometimes not accurate, so this exercise can help sort out participation patterns. I have seen this in my own work with teachers and in earlier research. Dale Spender (1982) videotaped teachers in high school classrooms, many of whom were "consciously trying to combat sexism" by calling on girls and boys equally. Upon reviewing the tapes and tallying the distribution of participation, the teachers were surprised that their perceived "overcorrection" of the unequal attention had only amounted to calling on the girls 35 percent of the time. The teachers reported that "giving the girls 35 percent of our time can feel as if we are being unfair to the boys." Although (we hope) the gender ratios in this research may be dated, the phenomenon of teacher misperception still holds. (For more on working with colleagues, see chapter 7.)

Teachers attending to participation patterns can use certain moves to encourage silent students to speak. For example, teachers might introduce a question with "Let's hear from somebody who hasn't spoken today." High-status students sometimes assert their standing by shooting their hands up when questions are posed, letting everybody know how quickly they know the answer. To get around this, teachers can pose a difficult question prefaced with the instructions, "No hands, just minds. I want all of you to think about this for the next minute. Look up at me when you think you know and I will call on somebody." By allowing thinking time, teachers value thoughtfulness over speed and have more opportunity to broaden participation. Eye contact between students and teacher is a subtle cue and will not disrupt others' thinking in the way that eagerly waving hands often do. Finally, teachers can make clear that they value partial answers as well as complete ones. When posing tough questions, they can say, "Even if you only have a little idea, tell us so we can have a starting place. It doesn't need to be all worked out."

Listening

Part of effective participation in classroom conversations requires listening and being heard. As a follow-up to an initial assessment of participation patterns, having an observer pay attention to *failed* bids for attention or to ideas that get dropped during a conversation might be useful.

Of course, part of the complexity of teaching is deciding which ideas to pursue and which ideas to table. But the choice of whether to entertain students' thinking communicates something to them about the value of their ideas, which ties directly to status. Students whose ideas are consistently taken up will have one impression about the value of their ideas; students whose ideas are consistently put off will have another idea entirely.

Teachers can model listening practices during class discussions, directing students to listen to each other. By showing students that rough-draft thinking—emergent, incompletely articulated ideas—is normal, teachers can help develop a set of clarifying questions that they ask students, and eventually, that students ask each other. For example, a teacher might say, "I'm not sure I follow. Could you please show me what you mean?" Saying this makes confusion a normal part of learning and communicates an expectation that students can demonstrate their thinking.

Body Language

During class, where are students focused? Are they looking at the clock or at the work on the table? Students who have their heads on the desk, hoodies pulled over their faces, or arms crossed while they gaze out a window are signaling nonparticipation. In small-group conversations, their chairs may be pulled back or their bodies turned away from the group. Body language can tell teachers a lot about students' engagement in a conversation.

Teachers' expectations for participation can include expectations about how students sit. "I want to see your eyes on your work, your bodies turned to your tables."

Organization of Materials and Resources

If students cannot see a shared problem during group work or put their hands on manipulatives, they cannot participate. If fat binders or mountains of backpacks obstruct their views of shared materials, they cannot participate. As with body language, teachers can make their expectation for the organization of materials explicit. "No binders or backpacks on your desks. All hands on the manipulatives."

Inflated Talk about Self or Others

Certain phrases or attitudes can be defeating and signal status problems. Adolescents often engage in teasing insults with each other, but such talk might become problematic in the classroom. Scrutinize judgments about other students' intelligence or the worthiness of their contributions. The statement "You always say such dumb things!" signals a status problem. "Gah! Why do you always do that?" might be more ambiguous. Teachers need to listen carefully and send clear messages about the importance of students treating each other with respect. "We disagree with ideas, not people" might be a helpful way to communicate this value.

Negative self-talk can be just as harmful. It not only reinforces students' impressions of themselves but also broadcasts these to others. "I'm so bad at math!" should be banned in the classroom. Give students other ways to express frustration: "I don't get this yet." The word *yet* is crucial because it communicates to students that their current level of understanding is not their endpoint. In fact, several teachers I know post *YET* on their walls so that any time a student makes a claim about not being able to do something, the teacher simply gestures to the word *YET* to reinforce the expectation that they will learn it eventually.

The converse of the negative self-talk issue also exists. If a student defends an idea only on the basis of his or her high status, this is a problem. Arguments should rest on mathematical justification, not social position. "Come on! Listen to me, I got an A on the last test" is not a valid warrant and should not be treated as one. By emphasizing the need for "becauses" or "statements and reasons" in mathematical discussions, teachers can winnow away arguments that rest on status.

The Opposite of Status Problems: Equal-Status Interactions

If students arrive in the classroom with expectations about whose contributions are worth listening to, they will act accordingly. They will solicit information and attend to the questions of high-status students. From a certain perspective, this *limited-exchange model* is an efficient way to get work done: go to the person who will have the information you need to complete the task.

In contrast, an *equal-exchange model* for working together serves different purposes, supporting all group members' engagement in higher-order thinking. Instead of a divide-and-conquer strategy with a goal of efficiency, equal exchanges involve deliberation and consideration of multiple perspectives with a goal of deeper understanding. When teachers want students to engage in conceptual learning and students are given a cognitively rich task, an equal-exchange model of interaction is vital.

Many teachers build in the expectation that students will learn to engage equitably even when students are engaged in less complex tasks. Teaching with the expectation that "no one is done until everyone is done" allows for this. Students begin to take responsibility for their own learning, as well as the need to support the learning of others in their group.

The first teaching challenge is to support students in shifting from limited to equal exchanges when they are working with rich mathematical tasks. Students need a purpose for soliciting the ideas of peers whom they may not expect to have worthwhile contributions. Teachers can cultivate equal-exchange or equal-status interactions in small groups by using two main strategies: structuring activities that necessitate group input (see chapter 4) and reworking students' assumptions about whose contributions are worthwhile. This latter strategy is the focus of this chapter.

In equal-status interactions, low-status students' participation and influence is not strongly distinguishable from that of their higher-status peers. Researchers Elizabeth Cohen and Rachel Lotan found that teachers' use of status treatments (see the Status Interventions section later) positively related to increased participation and influence of low-status students. Likewise, at the classroom level, the more teachers used status treatments, the less participation and influence were bound up in students' status (Cohen and Lotan 1995). In other words, equal-status interactions are the foundation of productive mathematical conversations.

Illustrations of Status Problems in Mathematics Classrooms

Status may be a useful concept to help teachers make sense of conversational breakdowns in their classroom as well as patterns of participation. The previous discussion highlighted specific signs of status problems, along with some ways to begin to address them, apart from any specific scenario. Of course, as status problems are embedded in particular interactions, untangling them gets trickier.

The following vignette is based on classroom observations in a school where teachers were learning to use complex instruction. More obvious examples of status problems exist, but I hope that the preceding discussion offers a way to identify egregiously problematic status dynamics. This excerpt presents a nuanced look at how status can operate in a group. Status may not be the first lens teachers might take to understand this interaction, but I suggest a status-based analysis to convince you that it might be a productive lens to increase participation in this classroom. Please take a moment to work out your thinking to the problem at the start of the vignette to better follow the students' conversations.

Vignette 3: Benign Dominance

The students in Ms. Munson's ninth-grade class are working in small groups on problems that require them to extrapolate data from linear graphs, build tables of values, and find rules. Jonah, Violetta, Ahmed, and Oliver sit around a table, working together.

Jonah and Oliver are European American and native English speakers. Ahmed is an African immigrant who speaks fluent English. Violetta is a Latina immigrant and less confident in her English.

After finding a table and a rule for a linear function with a positive slope, the group gets stuck on the following problem:

A family starts out with 100 pounds of flour. They use 10 pounds of flour every 5 days. How long will it take for them to run out of flour?

A graph accompanies the word problem, and the students have produced a table of values from the graph. They are having difficulty finding the corresponding equation.

Jonah articulates the trouble: "It *decreases*. It doesn't *increase*."

Oliver, watching Jonah closely, chimes in, "It decreases 20 pounds every 10 days."

Jonah says, "Or two pounds a day. But it *decreases*, so we can't multiply. Can we do division? I can't figure this out. We need to think of an equation for the amount of flour *gone*."

Jonah calls the teacher over and explains that "they" are perplexed by the decreasing function. She asks the group what kind of "special numbers" they might use to show that something is decreasing. Jonah tries out, "Fractions? Percents?"

Ms. Munson says, "What are we doing *every time*?"

Violetta answers, "Subtracting."

Ms. Munson nods. "So what kind of number can we use? Think about it."

Violetta: "Negatives?"

Ms. Munson nods. "Think about it. How can you use negatives to show our graph going down?" Then she walks away.

After she leaves, Jonah takes up the conversation again. "So it's going down 2 pounds a day. So, so . . . –2f times d, for days? It's like $y = mx + b$. Plus 100 because you start out with 100. Maybe 100x – 2f?"

Oliver asks, "100x – 2f what?"

Jonah responds, "f for flour; d for days."

Ahmed is listening with a frown on his face. "Let me try this. I got my calculator."

Jonah says, "So let's pick some data." He turns to the table that they have produced and tells Ahmed what to enter.

Ahmed finishes the calculation and says, "Nope. No, no. It doesn't work."

Jonah and Oliver groan. Violetta raises her head. She has been working away on her own during this conversation. "Do you guys have a rule?" she asks quietly.

The boys continue arguing over different arrangements of the numbers 100 and $-2f$ that might produce a correct equation.

Violetta then says, a little more forcefully, "I have an equation."

Jonah grabs her paper and puts it in the center of the table. "Let me see."

He reads from her paper, "$100 - d(2)$."

Ahmed grabs the paper. "Let me see!"

Violetta says quietly, "I tried it. It works."

Ahmed gets out his calculator and tests out an ordered pair. "She's right! She's smarter than I am."

The teacher comes by and the group shows her Violetta's equation. Ms. Munson asks, "Violetta, why don't you have an f in there?"

Violetta says, "Because you're talking about the days."

Ms. Munson asks her to explain it to her group. The boys still look surprised.

After Ms. Munson walks away, Violetta takes her paper back and tries to share her thinking. "We started out with 100 pounds, so we're going to need that number. Since we had 2 pounds of flour a day . . . How do you spell *flour*?"

Oliver spells it for her.

Violetta continues, "Since he says 2 pounds of flour in a day, I thought 100 subtracted . . . I don't know how to explain it."

Jonah's curiosity is not satisfied. "How'd you come up with it?"

Violetta says, "It's just the smartest thing to do. I just knew."

Ahmed says, "You used guess and check?"

Violetta: "No, I didn't check it." She pauses for a moment. "I got 100 because we started with 100. And since we're using the number of days, I put a d. And since the number of days is always 2 pounds of flour a day, I thought, well, d times 2. Two pounds of flour *per* day. But then we have to subtract it from how much we started with."

Jonah and the others look at her paper. Jonah says, "So d times 2. Very good." Then he applauds.

Analysis

In the preceding vignette, the group solves the problem and works through their mathematical confusion. Different students contribute to the solution. The students treat one another with respect. In a certain light, this is a successful instance of collaborative problem solving.

Nonetheless, issues of status are playing out in ways that might influence students' participation. Jonah, as the dominant speaker, appears to have the highest status in the group. We see this in how other students defer to him, as when Oliver repeats Jonah's assertion that "It *decreases*. It doesn't *increase*." Also, Jonah does not involve other students in sorting out the variables by soliciting their input. His talk focuses solely on his own ideas. When Ahmed, Oliver, and Violetta contribute, they have to make a bid to speak that he either allows or does not allow. Jonah's dominance may come from the other students' perceptions of him as smart, or it may come from his natural inclination to talk through his thinking.

Why does this matter at all, if ultimately the group solved the problem? Jonah's dominance here is a problem for several reasons. First, recall that while in class, students not only are learning mathematical content but also are developing their mathematical identities. Jonah's controlling the conversation reinforces the worthiness of his contributions over the others'. This situation could have been especially problematic if Violetta's good thinking had not been given a chance to be heard. (It almost didn't: Ms. Munson gave a two-minute warning just before Violetta raised her head and asked her groupmates whether they had found a rule. I wonder whether the teacher's calling time gave Violetta a sense of urgency about sharing her thinking and helped her gather the courage to do so.) Yet Violetta had the key insight in constructing the equation: the input of the function is *days*, not *pounds of flour* as Jonah had formulated.

Recall equity principle 4: *Students need to see themselves in mathematics.* While they learn mathematical content, students are also learning who they are in relation to mathematics during a class session. This awareness influences their persistence on hard problems and future engagement in the subject. Why should they continue, on this problem or in this content area, if they know that they are not good at it? If their ideas or questions are ignored, students will not see themselves in mathematics. For these reasons, status plays heavily into this equity principle.

Teachers do not always know the source of students' status within a group. We cannot necessarily discern whether Violetta's prior achievement, accented English, brown skin, or gender led the boys in her group not to seek out her ideas. Instead of assuming that students' characteristics *necessarily* indicate their status, cautious teachers recognize that class, race, gender, and language fluency *might* signal status to their peers but wait to observe how these play out in interaction. Sometimes individuals bear the burden of negative stereotypes about their intellectual ability on the basis of their social groups—a phenomenon called *stereotype threat* (Aronson 2004) that makes people reluctant to speak and confirm these assumptions. Sometimes these stereotypes are not in play. In this vignette, for instance, Ahmed, an African immigrant, participated more confidently than Oliver by taking on the job of equation checking.

Status Interventions

When status plays out in the complex world of the classroom, it takes many shapes. Although blatant dominance, insults, or nonparticipation are easy to spot, the more subtle manifestations take skill to identify and remedy. Effectively intervening with status problems first requires analysis of the situation. Figuring out the best strategy for remedying the problem is often a trial-and-error process. Teachers get better at managing status in their classrooms over time, but even accomplished teachers run into challenges that force them to further sharpen their intervention tools.

The following strategies outline a starting point for status interventions. Unfortunately, this is not a recipe that will make status problems magically disappear. Status will always be part of our social world. The trick is to manage it such that students begin to reimagine themselves and their peers in the context of their competence and not their deficits. Every class you teach will have different personalities and dynamics, so these will play out differently in each circumstance. Nonetheless, here are some tested status interventions that can be adapted to any classroom.

Establishing and Maintaining Norms

Effective classroom norms support equal-status interactions. (This is one place where the CI practice I learned from the teachers differs from the CI research. The teachers I worked with felt that effective norms could actually curtail status problems. The research of Elizabeth Cohen et al. suggests that norms do not affect status problems; it is really status treatments and multiple-ability orientations that do.) In the previous discussion of status problems, I suggested some structures teachers can use, such as "no hands, just minds," that help curb status problems. These all communicate norms for participating and interacting. For our purposes, I will use the following definition of norms:

> *Classroom norms are agreed-upon ways of behaving.*

Establishing norms requires a conversation with students. Some teachers do this interactively, asking students to contribute their answers to the question, "What makes you comfortable in a classroom?" Other teachers let students know that they have found certain behaviors helpful in making a positive classroom environment where students feel comfortable to learn. However they are arrived at, posting a list of norms on the wall as a reminder can help keep these at the forefront.

Norms can help curb status problems. For example, establishing the norm of *no put-downs* can minimize negative talk about oneself or others. The YET sign is another means of establishing the norm that everybody can learn over time. Examples of other norms that help support equal status interactions include the following:

- *Take turns.*

- *Listen to others' ideas.*

- *Disagree with ideas, not people.*

- *Be respectful.*

- *Helping is not the same as giving answers.*

- *Confusion is part of learning.*

- *Say your "becauses."*

Because norms are associated with classroom behavior, they are often thought of as a classroom management tool. In a sense, they are, but they go beyond that. Classroom management is often understood as serving the important goal of managing the crowd in the classroom. Students may or may not value that goal. The use of norms as I describe them *helps students learn.*

To make norms more relevant to students, always link norms to your learning goals. For example, *helping is not the same as giving answers* values explanations and learning over the completion of work. Similarly, *say your "becauses"* values the mathematical work of justification over assertions of correct answers that may be based in status. This norm also helps alleviate the problem of nonmathematical assertion of an argument by helping a lower-status student demand that a higher-status student better explain an assertion. In classrooms where this norm is in use, I hear students say to one another, "Yeah, but *why*? You didn't say your 'because.'"

Telling students expectations for acceptable behavior does not, of course, ensure that they will always meet them. Norms require maintenance. New situations might create a need to reestablish them. Even new content—particularly content that highlights differences in prior achievement—can heighten status issues and therefore require a strong reminder about classroom norms.

Addressing Status through Norms

Over time, teachers get better at analyzing which norms might help shift negative status dynamics in their classrooms. Teachers pick one or two norms for a particular activity and tell students, "While you are working on this, I am going to watch how you do on these norms." The teacher then reminds students of the expectation for acceptable behavior.

Sometimes the choice of norms comes from a teacher's reading of the dynamics in prior class sessions. For example, if student conversations are coming too close to personal attacks, a teacher might highlight the norms *be respectful* and *disagree with ideas, not people.* If the teacher then circulates around the room and reminds students of these norms, he is not picking on problem students; rather, the teacher is stating a classroom goal that everybody is trying to work on.

Likewise, teachers can predict mathematical activities that might lead to status problems and use norms to head these off. Any topic that is confusing may make students vulnerable to status concerns. Reminding students that *confusion is a part of learning* can help. I have heard teachers say, "Now, I don't expect you to get this problem quickly. It's really hard and you will need each other's help. If you get confused, that's great because it means you are learning."

Sometimes, specific topics expose students' status concerns. Calculations with fractions commonly bring out insecurity in previously low-achieving students and impatience in students who are already fluent in these calculations: a recipe for a status collision. Anticipating this, a teacher can let the class know that she will be watching for the norms *helping is not the same as giving answers* and *say your "becauses."* The first norm will send a clear message that students who can calculate quickly need to do more than show the other students their answers. The second norm offers less confident students a means to demand explanations from their peers ("Okay, but you didn't say the 'because'").

Multiple-Ability Treatment

So far, this discussion of status has acknowledged the different status levels of students in any classroom and how it can undermine productive mathematical conversations. No doubt, addressing status through norms is crucial to creating equal-status interactions. By helping students interact more productively—listening respectfully, justifying their thinking—we help support meaningful mathematical conversations.

Norms, however, will take us only so far. Unless we address underlying conceptions of smartness, we risk reverting to the commonly held belief that group work benefits struggling students because smart students help them. As long as we have a simplistic view of some students as smart and others as struggling, we will have status problems in our classrooms. Students quickly pick up on assessments of their ability. For example, when teachers arrange collaborative groups to evenly distribute strong, weak, and average students, children will figure out that scheme and rapidly learn which slot they fill. No doubt, learners benefit from seeing more expert performance and should have opportunities to do so. But if we value only certain kinds of expertise, the same students will always play the role of experts. The question then becomes, What kinds of mathematical competence have a place in your classroom activities? If the mathematics is rich enough, the strengths of different students will come into play, rendering the common mixed-ability grouping strategy useless. Ordering the students by achievement and evenly distributing *strong, weak,* and *average* students across the groups will no longer be enough.

	Team Captain	Recorder	Facilitator	Resource Monitor
Team 1	Abby	Brian	Jeff	Alene
Team 2	Adam	Andrea	Melanie	Emily
Team 3	Lisa	Rich	Lee	Doug
Team 4	Cliff	Brenda	Deb	Kevin
Team 5	Sandra	Nick	Bridget	Mike
Team 6	Paul	Hugo	Jackie	David
Team 7	Anne	Kathy	Angie	JJ

Fig. 3.1. A wall-hanging seating chart to organize group assignments

In fact, an essential practice for a multiple-ability classroom is *random group assignment*. If we believe that students can all learn from each other, then group assignments should have no underlying design based on assessments of ability. Teachers often do this by using a wall-hanging seating chart that has pockets for each student's name (fig. 3.1). When it is time to rearrange groups, they will shuffle the cards and simply redistribute them in the pockets to make a transparent show of the randomness of group assignments. If a teacher judges a certain pairing of students to be unwise, she can publicly state the reason for this (e.g., "You two tend to get too silly together, so I think I will switch you out"). These reasons are not judgments about smartness but are instead social considerations. Random group assignment, however, is just one component of multiple-ability treatments.

Another component of multiple-ability treatments involves reconsidering what being mathematically competent means. In schools, the most valued kind of mathematical competence is typically quick and accurate calculation. A facility with numbers and algorithms no doubt reflects important mathematical proclivities. To broaden participation in our classroom in an authentically mathematical way, however, we need to broaden our notions of what mathematical competence looks like.

In the history of mathematics, mathematical competencies other than quick and accurate calculation have helped develop the field. For example, Fermat's Last Theorem was posed as a question that seemed worth entertaining for more than three centuries because of its compelling intuitiveness. When Andrew Wiles's solution came in the late twentieth century, it rested on the insightful connection he made between two seemingly disparate topics: number theory and elliptical curves. Hyperbolic geometry became a convincing alternative system for representing space because of Poincaré's ingenious half-plane and disk models, which helped provide a means for constructions and visualizations in this non-Euclidean space. When the controversy over multiple geometries brewed, Klein's Erlangen program developed an axiomatic system that helped explain the logic and relationships among these seemingly irreconcilable models. In the 1970s, Kenneth Appel and Wolfgang Haken's proof of the Four Color Theorem was hotly debated because of its innovative use of computers to systematically consider every possible case. When aberrations have come up over the years, such as irrational or imaginary numbers, ingenious mathematicians have extended systems of calculation to encompass them so that they become number systems in their own right.

This glimpse into the history of mathematics shows that multiple competencies propel mathematical discovery:

- posing interesting questions (Fermat);

- making astute connections (Wiles);

- representing ideas clearly (Poincaré);

- developing logical explanations (Klein);

- working systematically (Appel and Haken); and

- extending ideas (irrational/complex number systems).

These are all vital mathematical competencies. Surprisingly, students have few opportunities to recognize these competencies in themselves or their peers while in school. Our system highlights the competence of calculating quickly and accurately, sometimes at the expense of other competencies that require a different pace of problem solving.

Evaluating people on one dimension of mathematical competence ranks students from most to least competent. This rank order usually relates to students' academic status, and students tend to be aware of it. One way to interrupt status is to recognize multiple mathematical abilities. Instead of a one-dimensional rank order, we create a multidimensional competence space. Although some students may have multiple mathematical competencies, more places in which to get better surely exist. Likewise, a student who ranks low on the hierarchy produced when we focus on quick and accurate calculation may have a real strength at making astute connections, working systematically, or representing ideas clearly. We cannot address status hierarchies without emphasizing multiple mathematical competencies in the classroom.

A multiple-ability classroom represents a dramatic shift in the topography of mathematical ability. Instead of lining students up in a row in order of smartness, a multiple-ability classroom has students standing on different peaks and valleys of a hilly multidimensional terrain. No one student is always clearly above another. This structure may unsettle students who are used to being on top, as well as those whose vantage points and contributions have been presumed less valuable. In other words, challenging the status hierarchy by developing a multiple-ability view can provoke strong emotions from students, positive and negative. Teachers should not be surprised to see this response in their classrooms.

In chapter 4, I will discuss choosing and adapting tasks to encompass multiple abilities. If teachers have a rich mathematical task, they can head off status problems by carrying out a multiple-ability treatment (Cohen 1994). A multiple-ability treatment comes in the launch of a task. After presenting the directions and expectations, teachers list the specific mathematical abilities that students will need for the task and add the phrase, "No one of us has all of these abilities, so you will need each other to get this work done." By publicly acknowledging the need for more than just quick and accurate calculation, teachers offer an in for a broader range of students. Multiple-ability treatments do other work too, particularly fostering interdependence. I will discuss this in more detail in chapter 5.

Assigning Competence

> "Assigning competence is the hardest aspect of CI to do well, but by far the most essential. I had to be honest with myself about my assumptions about what it means to be smart, and push myself to expand that definition in ways I genuinely believed. I had to train myself to have eyes and ears for smartness when it happened, and also the vocabulary to name it. I need to be able to assign competence every time a student presents at the overhead, and every time I work with a team."
>
> —*Carlos Cabana, Complex Instruction Educator and Mathematics Teacher*

The two status interventions described so far operate on the classroom level. Norms give clear expectations for behavior to push students toward more productive mathematical conversations. Multiple-ability treatments highlight teachers' valuing of broader mathematical competencies.

The next step is to help students recognize where they and their classmates are located on the complex topography of mathematical competence to shift their self-concept and their ideas about others. Students need to recognize these other competencies for themselves so that they know their own strengths and can work confidently on hard problems. They need to recognize the strengths of their peers in order to interrupt assumptions based on a simplistic smartness hierarchy. If students believe their classmates have something to contribute, they have a mathematically motivated reason to listen to and learn from each other.

Teachers can communicate these messages to students through the practice of *assigning competence*.

> *Assigning competence is a form of praise where teachers catch students being smart. The praise is* public, specific to the task, *and* intellectually meaningful.

The *public* part of assigning competence means that this praise is not an aside to an individual student or a communication with the parent. It takes place in the public realm of the classroom, whether in small-group activity or whole-class discussion. It needs to be *specific to the task* so that students make a connection between their behavior and their mathematical contribution. Simply saying, "Good job!" is not enough. Students need to know exactly what they did that is valued. The praise must be *intellectually meaningful* so that it contributes to students' sense of smartness. Praising a student for a "beautiful poster" does not qualify as assigning competence, because making a beautiful poster does not display mathematical intellect. In contrast, if a teacher praises a student for a clear representation on a poster that helps explain an idea, that is intellectually meaningful because it is tied to mathematics.

In the vignette, for example, if Ms. Munford had noticed Violetta's good thinking on the problem, she could have *assigned her competence* by making it public to either the group or possibly even the class. She could say, "Wow, Violetta! Your group was having trouble figuring out the equation. That was great how you recognized that D was the unknown. That was a really important connection." If she wanted to do more to bring Violetta's groupmates into the status treatment, Ms. Munford could add, "Jonah, Ahmed, and Oliver, make sure to get Violetta's ideas in there. She's got some good insights!"

> "If I were to have a teacher concentrate on one aspect of CI, it would be to focus on learning how your students are smart and how they are developing confidence in their learning of mathematics and their encouragement of each other."
> —*Ruth Tsu, Retired Mathematics Teacher and Complex Instruction Educator*

Summary

Status plays into teachers' and students' ability to have productive mathematical conversations in their classrooms, at both the whole-class and small-group levels. Status is based on judgments of worthiness that arise from prior academic achievement and social desirability. Patterns of participation and nonparticipation (or even marginalization) signal whose contributions are valued in a particular classroom. Status problems interrupt productive mathematical conversations because speakers' ideas are entertained or discounted on social rather than mathematical grounds. Figure 3.2 represents the influence of status on students' mathematical learning.

Teachers can address status problems in the classroom in several ways (fig. 3.3). Most fundamentally, teachers need to establish classroom norms that value respectful listening and the use of mathematical practices, such as justifying as the grounds for discussion. Teachers establish norms through initial conversation with students but then must maintain the norms by aligning conversational practices with stated values. Teachers can target specific norms to respond to or head off status problems in their classrooms.

As long as linear views of mathematical competence exist, norms will not sufficiently address status problems in the classroom. To broaden student participation, teachers must authentically extend views of smartness in their classroom. Typically, quick and accurate calculation is the primary mathematical competence valued in school. Other forms of competence, such as making key connections or working systematically, happen over more than one class session—but mathematics classrooms often obscure these. To help students understand their own mathematical competencies, teachers can also disrupt status problems by assigning competence to students. Assigning competence is a particular form of praise that is public, specific, and intellectually meaningful and can help shift students' perceptions of the value of their own and others' contributions.

In the next chapter, we will extend these ideas and explore the nature of mathematical tasks that support broadened notions of smartness.

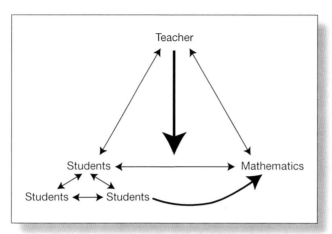

Fig. 3.2. Students' interactions with each other influence their access to mathematics.

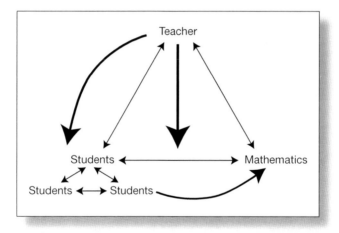

Fig. 3.3. Teachers can actively shift the dynamic among students by using status interventions, supporting equal-status interactions in small groups.

Providing Access to Meaningful Mathematics: Groupworthy Tasks

So far, I have introduced several ideas that aim to shift our thinking about what teaching secondary mathematics means. In chapter 1, I argue that, to encompass all that children learn in school, we need to move away from a notion of teaching as *effective presentation of ideas* toward a view of teaching as *designing effective learning environments*. In chapter 2, I discussed equity and offered four interpretive principles teachers can use to make learning environments more equitable. In chapter 3, I introduced *status* and described how it influences mathematical learning and how teachers can cultivate equal-status interactions through valuing different kinds of mathematical smartness.

Two things are worth noting here. First, although the vignettes in earlier chapters portray group work, the application of these main ideas extends beyond small-group settings. This is because group work as a learning environment is embedded in other aspects of instruction. Second, while I have hinted at an underlying conception of content, I have not yet fully explained what the mathematics itself might look like in an equitable classroom that uses collaborative learning effectively.

Just as I proposed in earlier chapters different ways of looking at the classroom, teaching, and students, I develop here a perspective on mathematics compatible with equitable collaborative learning. The shift can be characterized as one that goes from *ready-made mathematics* to *mathematics in the making* (the latter based on studies of scientists at work, described in Latour [1997]). That is, instead of having children learn what has already been figured out, we teach children mathematical content through sense making so that they learn not only *how* to do mathematics but also *why* it works. In this chapter, I will describe how this broader view of mathematics supports equitable group work.

Broadening Mathematics

Rigor and accessibility are often viewed as competing goals in mathematics teaching. The concept may seem paradoxical at first, but increasing rigor actually can support greater access. The resolution of the paradox comes from the particular strategy for broadening content. Some may bristle at the idea of broadening mathematics, assuming that doing so entails watering down the subject. Instead, by expanding school mathematics to make it more closely resemble the work of mathematicians, we deepen the integrity of the content and simultaneously make it more accessible.

The shift toward mathematics in the making is a move toward *mathematical proficiency*. This form of mathematical competence has five strands (Kilpatrick, Swafford, and Findell 2001, p. 5):

1. *Conceptual understanding*—comprehension of mathematical concepts, operations, and relations

2. *Procedural fluency*—skill in carrying out procedures flexibly, accurately, efficiently, and appropriately

3. *Strategic competence*—ability to formulate, represent, and solve mathematical problems

4. *Adaptive reasoning*—capacity for logical thought, reflection, explanation, and justification

5. *Productive disposition*—habitual inclination to see mathematics as sensible, useful, and worthwhile, coupled with a belief in diligence and one's own efficacy.

When students can demonstrate these forms of mathematical thinking, they do more than just learn mathematics. They can do mathematics. This vision of content aligns well with the rich mathematical learning environments that support equitable collaborative learning.

Researchers Magdalene Lampert and Deborah Ball conducted some of the first teaching experiments seeking to bring mathematics in the making into elementary school classrooms. Unlike earlier attempts to bring authentic mathematical thinking into the classroom, Lampert and Ball paid close attention not only to the structure of the content but also to how children learned mathematical ideas. Their rich classroom records, which include videotapes of daily lessons, lesson plans, teacher journals, and student work, have yielded enduring images of what teaching mathematical thinking might look like (Lampert and Ball 1998).

Important mathematical practices in their classrooms included reasoning, justification, building definitions and representations, and reconciling seemingly different approaches to problems. These mathematical thinking practices are the key to bringing deeper content while supporting greater access to sense making. Figure 4.1 illustrates some of the mathematical habits of mind that can enrich classroom learning.

Some Key Ideas about Mathematical Learning

Lampert and Ball's work was pivotal in helping teachers envision what might be possible in mathematics classrooms. Thanks to their work and the work of other mathematics education researchers, we know a lot more about how people learn mathematics since the first NCTM *Standards* were written in the late 1980s. *Principles and Standards for School Mathematics* reflects much of this research (NCTM 2000; Kilpatrick, Martin, and Schifter 2003).

Here are some key ideas from this research:

- *To use knowledge flexibly, students need to understand what they are learning.* Recitation and memorization generally allow students to develop a limited mathematical competence. They may be able to produce an answer when given a similar question to one that they have seen, but they are often stumped when they need to use their knowledge in new situations. Also, when students learn ideas superficially, they tend not to retain them.

- *New understandings build off prior understandings.* Students do not come to mathematics classes as blank slates. They have a set of experiences, intuitions, and ideas about number and space. Effective teaching requires that these prior understandings be engaged in the classroom. The metaphor of a *scaffold* is often used to describe how teachers might start with students' conceptions of a topic and build toward conventional mathematical understandings. To be valuable, scaffolds must engage students' understandings, not simply wallpaper over them.

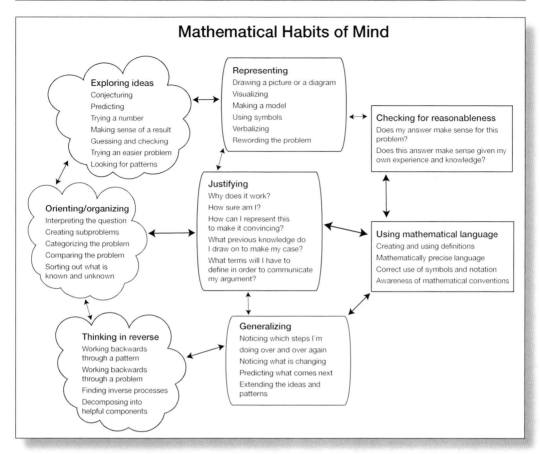

Mathematical Habits of Mind

Exploring ideas
Conjecturing
Predicting
Trying a number
Making sense of a result
Guessing and checking
Trying an easier problem
Looking for patterns

Representing
Drawing a picture or a diagram
Visualizing
Making a model
Using symbols
Verbalizing
Rewording the problem

Checking for reasonableness
Does my answer make sense for this problem?
Does this answer make sense given my own experience and knowledge?

Orienting/organizing
Interpreting the question
Creating subproblems
Categorizing the problem
Comparing the problem
Sorting out what is known and unknown

Justifying
Why does it work?
How sure am I?
How can I represent this to make it convincing?
What previous knowledge do I draw on to make my case?
What terms will I have to define in order to communicate my argument?

Using mathematical language
Creating and using definitions
Mathematically precise language
Correct use of symbols and notation
Awareness of mathematical conventions

Thinking in reverse
Working backwards through a pattern
Working backwards through a problem
Finding inverse processes
Decomposing into helpful components

Generalizing
Noticing which steps I'm doing over and over again
Noticing what is changing
Predicting what comes next
Extending the ideas and patterns

Fig. 4.1. Some mathematical habits of mind, along with the mathematical activities or questions that support their development

- *Mathematical practices such as argumentation and justification support student understanding.* Argumentation, justification, and generalization are thinking practices that mathematicians engage in. They also support students' understandings of content by helping them learn not just the *how* of mathematics but also the *why*. Argumentation and justification support the scaffolding of student thinking because asking students to justify their thinking requires engagement of their prior understandings.

- *Students need to be encouraged to see themselves as a source of mathematical knowledge.* One great feature of mathematics as a subject is that it makes sense. If its underlying principles are understood, others can be deduced. If students lose sight of the underlying logic, they take an approach of memorizing from a textbook. Although this approach may help them pass tests or do problems that are closely related to the ones they practice on, they typically become paralyzed when they encounter a slightly different problem. They also forget what they have learned too quickly. If students know how to reason mathematically, they can often think their way through difficult problems and better retain information. This is where mathematical proficiency comes in.

- *How students learn influences cognition, motivation, affect, and sense of self.* We live in an era that focuses mainly on the cognitive outcomes of learning. Classroom teachers must contend with the interrelated issues of motivation, affect, and self-concept. A learning environment perspective on teaching helps make sense of these other dimensions of instruction, because the contexts of learning influence students' learning of content. For example, they influence students' persistence on difficult problems and in the subject over time, as well as their feelings about mathematics, including contributing to or detracting from math anxiety. As we discussed in chapter 3, the status dimension of classroom interactions can profoundly affect how students think of themselves as mathematics learners.

New Ideas, New Dilemmas

Most educators would not argue against the idea of teaching for understanding. Intuitively, people usually realize that they learn better and have more flexible knowledge when they have a deep understanding of an idea. To teach with this goal in mind certainly requires a departure from the traditional mathematics classrooms described in chapter 1. Teaching mathematics for understanding poses new challenges.

For instance, how do we build off the prior knowledge of thirty people in one classroom? Getting a handle on *one* student's understandings of a single curricular topic can be challenging enough. Also, how is a lone teacher to do this for every student in every class for every topic, when secondary teachers teach five or six sections a day? Likewise, when we dig into student understandings, we might stumble upon gaping holes in their knowledge base, which leads to a new dilemma. Do we follow the students or follow the curriculum?

Although complex instruction cannot entirely resolve these dilemmas, effective small-group learning can help address some of these tensions for teachers. To achieve efficacy, we first must address some common assumptions about mathematical learning.

Mathematics Is a Group of Connected Ideas

To productively direct students' sense making, teachers need to shift away from a primarily hierarchical view of mathematics to a connected view. Although we tend to think of mathematics as progressing in a sequence, with students needing to wholly master prerequisite skills before they can learn new ones, this is often not the case. To be clear: mathematics certainly has a logical deductive structure, yet nobody would propose teaching out of the *Principia Mathematica*. (The *Principia Mathematica* is a three-volume work on the foundations of mathematics, written by Alfred North Whitehead and Bertrand Russell and published in the early twentieth century. It sought to derive all mathematical truths from a set of axioms by using logical deduction.) Bringing this point closer to secondary content: understanding algebra before having gained fluency in multiplication facts might be difficult, but there is no reason why students cannot develop the concept of variable and inverse operations to solve equations *while* they work on their computational fluency in multiplication. Although teachers need to respond to gaps in student knowledge, the missing pieces do not necessarily require a complete reteaching of older topics.

Mathematics Is Not Strictly Hierarchical

The opposite of a *connected view* of mathematics is a *hierarchical view*. In this perspective, mathematics is a sequence of topics that necessarily build off one another. In traditional secondary mathematics curricula, this sequence culminates in the study of calculus. A connected view of mathematics, in contrast, emphasizes the discipline's big ideas and what have been referred to as *habits of mind* (Cuoco, Goldenberg, and Mark 1996). In the algebra example, helping students develop a concept of variable and of inverse operations emphasizes understanding strategies for equation solving. Big ideas are generalizable and appear throughout the study of mathematics. Inverse operations simply point to the mathematical habit of mind that Mark Driscoll (1999) refers to as *doing–undoing:* anything we do in mathematics, we seek to undo. This premise holds true for arithmetic operations as well as for functions in calculus and linear transformations in groups. The principle extends beyond the specific topic of study, so it is generative for students' future mathematical learning.

The increase in mathematical rigor comes from bringing school mathematics closer in line with mathematics itself. The broader notion of mathematics itself provides an important shift for the success of complex instruction. By incorporating *more* mathematical skills in our teaching, we give students more opportunities to demonstrate competence. These different mathematical skills are the source of the multiple abilities that allow us to address status in our classroom.

Turning Some Pet Ideas about Mathematics Teaching on Their Heads

Before we construct tasks that will support collaborative learning, we must first challenge a few pet ideas about mathematics teaching. Certain mathematical teaching practices come from the hierarchical view of the subject. When we shift to a connected view, we select and organize tasks differently. Doing so is particularly important for successful group work.

Start with Challenging Stuff, Not Easy Stuff

Classroom mathematics tasks tend to be organized so that a simple example is presented first, followed by similar problems that gradually get harder. The problem set may or may not culminate in a challenge problem.

What's wrong with this approach? On the surface, it makes sense. If learners are anxious, we want to build their confidence by allowing them the opportunity to be successful. In collaborative learning, though, this approach is a disaster for several reasons. By presenting a problem that maps easily onto an example, teachers inadvertently encourage students who see patterns quickly to take over the task without involving their groupmates. Because good pattern seers tend to succeed in school mathematics, this structure supports their ongoing dominance and reinforces existing status problems. Also, leaving the meaty problems for the end may deprive many students from ever getting to the substantive content. In fact, some students believe challenge problems are optional or "only for the smart kids." Well-chosen challenge problems serve as a good starting point for group work *because* they help students get directly to the heart of mathematical issues. Finally, by starting with challenging problems, teachers send the message that all students can engage with difficult content, especially when students have each other as resources. Repeated experience with difficult problems supports students' development of the kinds of strategies that strengthen their mathematical reasoning.

In sum, starting with the easy stuff contributes to inequitable teaching. Putting challenging content at the end of assignments limits who has opportunities to engage with these problems and, in doing so, perpetuates the opportunity gaps that limit student learning. In addition, making challenging problems essentially optional means that many students are not pushed to learn mathematics more deeply.

Effective Group Learning Allows All Learners to Help Each Other

I often hear teachers talk about collaborative learning as offering opportunities for "fast learners" to slow down and teach, while struggling learners get in-class tutoring from their peers.

This usual way of thinking about collaborative learning contributes to status problems. As I said in chapter 3, students quickly size up any underlying design of your groupings. They will recognize if they are being put in the "smart one" or "minority student" slot, and they will often act accordingly. Productive mathematical conversations weigh arguments on the basis of mathematical validity, not on who is speaking. The very act of putting students in slots assigns them a role linked to their presumed competence, socially endowing them with different levels of authority regardless of what they say. Likewise, if we truly create a multiple-ability classroom centered on problems that require a range of mathematical skills, then the added dimensions of mathematical competence should scramble any hierarchical ranking of student ability.

Using Groupworthy Mathematical Tasks

Complex instruction requires a thoughtful design of mathematical activities. Not all classroom work is well suited for collaborative learning. To distinguish between tasks that are and are not, teachers have developed the idea of *groupworthy tasks*.

To illustrate this concept, I will take a problem that has these properties and explain how you might use it to make it groupworthy. Take a moment to look at the task (fig. 4.2) and think through how you might do it. Then think about what students might do.

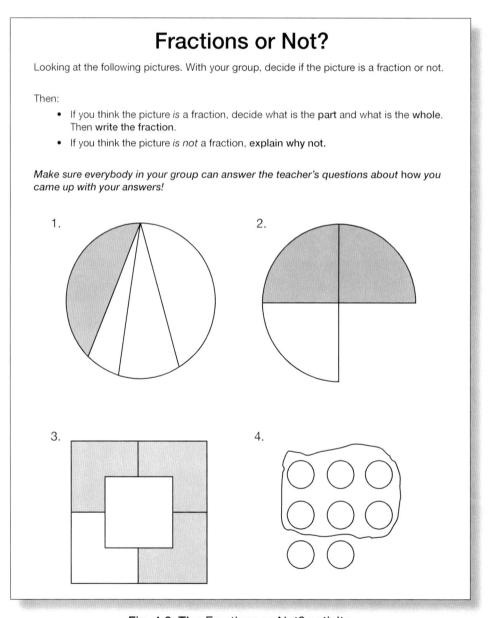

Fig. 4.2. The *Fractions or Not?* activity

Groupworthy tasks have six common features (Lotan 2003). To be groupworthy, a task needs to do the following:

- *Focus on central mathematical concepts or ideas.* Once we shift our thinking about mathematics from a sequence of topics to a network of ideas, we can identify which ones are important to teach. (For more resources on processes that help identify what is important to teach, see Wiggins and McTighe [2005].) In general, they are the topics that students will encounter again and again, that support long-term understanding of the content, and that illuminate important concepts. Our goal is to help students develop important insights about these ideas so that they can use them flexibly in a variety of contexts, in our class and in the future.

  As all secondary-level mathematics teachers know, computations with fractions are the downfall of many U.S. citizens. The mere presence of a fraction can petrify some students. This activity helps students revisit the definition of fractions and asks them to apply it to nonstandard diagrams. The teacher who shared this task with me had a goal of working on conceptual fraction problems in her class to ensure that everybody had a good grasp of what fractions were, providing a conceptual resource for them to use in other nonstandard problem contexts.

- *Require some interpretation.* Groupworthy tasks incorporate multiple intellectual abilities. To support equal-status interactions in small-group contexts, teachers need to disrupt classroom status hierarchies. Doing that is possible only if students have intellectually meaningful ways to contribute different perspectives to a task. The *Fractions or Not?* task requires multiple abilities. To work on this activity successfully, students need to use the definition of a fraction and apply it to nonstandard contexts. Diagram 2, in particular, pushes students to reconsider a familiar shape—a 90° sector of a circle, which usually represents ¼—and understand why in this situation it is actually ⅓. To see this, students need to be able to reinterpret visual cues and make arguments for their interpretation of the different diagrams.

- *Provide multiple ways of being competent in problem solving.* Sometimes when teachers are first using complex instruction, they think that long or multistep problems qualify as groupworthy. This second criterion of groupworthiness is important because it sets the stage for students' discussion. Students at a broad range of achievement levels should have a way into the problem. Diagram 3, in particular, is fruitful for student discussion because it can be looked at in two different ways. Either the white square in the middle can be seen as *part* of the whole or it can be viewed as empty space, leaving the other four L-shaped parts as the whole. I have seen students passionately debate the nature of this diagram, carefully invoking the definition of fractions in the process. Creating an open-ended task like this that forces student interpretations allows discussion of different approaches, creating a context for students' justification of their thinking and the reconciliation of diverse conceptions.

- *Be done in a group, which bolsters students' interdependence.* A well-known issue with collaborative learning comes when one student takes over the cognitive work of a task while the other students sit back and socialize. To eliminate this free-rider effect, teachers need to ensure that tasks actually *require* the input of multiple students to work effectively. (I will talk more about fostering interdependence in chapter 5.)

  A single student working on this problem would not see all the different possible ways to interpret the diagrams, and therefore the underlying concepts would not necessarily surface. This problem works *better* in groups than it would alone. Also, the nonstandard diagrams force a considered interpretation, slowing students down and pushing them to reassess their automatic responses.

- *Be designed in a way that provides individual and group accountability.* Related to the concern about students' simply using others' thinking without doing any of their own, accountability systems need to be in place that require all students to contribute. I will get into more detail about accountability strategies in chapter 5, but I will present one example here to illustrate. Classroom routines are one way to communicate norms and expectations, including ones involving accountability. In many complex-instruction classrooms, teachers answer *group questions* only during collaborative learning time. If a group of students calls the teacher over, the teacher will ask, "Is this a group question?" If not, the teacher says, "Ask each other first, and then if you still don't know, I will come back." If the students answer affirmatively, the teacher will then call on *any* student to state the question. The group question routine increases mutual accountability and individual accountability. Students cannot get their individual questions answered without first discussing them with their group. If the teacher's help is still needed, each student must be prepared to articulate the question and answer the teacher's follow-up questions about it.

- *Have clear evaluation criteria.* Clear evaluation criteria are essential to any good assessment. Articulating to students what you are looking for makes your expectations visible to students. It supports the goal of autonomy because it allows students to know whether they have fulfilled the requirements of the task. It also provides consistency across groups of students. Evaluation criteria should be written in language that students can understand, and should inform them about what constitutes exemplary work. For example, "An outstanding poster will have the problem statement, your strategy, a solution statement, and a clear justifications for your reasoning. Students from other groups should be able to walk up to your poster and understand what you did." For a smaller task such as *Fractions or Not?*, teachers might have simpler goals, such as, "Anyone in your group should be able to explain your answers to my questions when I check your work. Make sure you have *reasons* for your answers." Clear evaluation criteria support more focused and higher quality student discussions, as well as better final products (Cohen and Lotan 2003).

> "We know that students often walk into our math classes filled with fear but also with hope. Math has caused them to feel stupid in the past, but they are hoping that this year, with this teacher, will be different. More than anything else, the tools of [complex instruction] have helped me face this enormous responsibility. For example, an emphasis on groupworthy tasks means that I am asking students to work on harder mathematics — harder because I am asking them to justify, use multiple representations, generalize, connect, apply, and reverse processes. This lets me catch more students being smart and challenge every student to work on getting smarter."
>
> —*Carlos Cabana, Complex Instruction Educator and Mathematics Teacher*

Other Notes about Task Design

Finding a groupworthy problem poses the first challenge to organizing content. Usually, problems need to be reformatted to make them suitable to group work. One dilemma of group work is that, to air their conceptions, students in groups need some autonomy from the teacher. But teachers cannot simply turn the conversations over to students without significant forethought. Teachers need to ensure that student conversations center on important ideas in the curriculum. One tool for managing this delegation of authority is the *task card* that teachers distribute to groups. A task card supports group autonomy by giving students the problem to have at their tables, not just at the board. It differs from a worksheet by giving guidance for the activity, but it is not meant for students to write on or turn in. Giving two cards to a group of four or five students forces students to share resources, another way to foster interdependence. Some teachers put their task cards in plastic sleeves to reuse them for multiple class sessions.

Because we want students to work during their collaborative time with as little teacher intervention as possible, thought must go into some of the details of the task card design. Here are some things to think about in designing a task card:

- *Layout.* Ideally, the task should be clearly laid out, with a set of simple directions and diagrams. Task cards should use an appropriate font size and include a clear sequence of directions, diagrams, probing questions, and evaluation criteria. Take care not to proceduralize the task, however. Leaving some ambiguity gives students something to talk about.

- *Language.* A mathematical task should not become a reading comprehension exercise. Problems need to be simply stated. Most word processing programs have an easy way to check for the reading level of any text you produce. Aim for two grade levels below your students' grade. Doing so may require finding words with fewer syllables and breaking text into shorter sentences. Be mindful of English language learners, and note any mathematical language or problem contexts that might be unfamiliar.

- *Representations.* Diagrams, number lines, and graphs are some representations that are central to mathematics. Not only do they potentially push students' thinking, but they might also serve as a resource for students who are good visual thinkers. Also, English language learners might be able to make sense of a problem using diagrams or manipulatives more successfully than they could a standard word problem.

- *Evaluation criteria.* On a task card, communicate to students what you are looking for, either on their written work or in their conversations. Doing so lets students know that they are all individually accountable for the group's thinking and emphasizes the teacher's interest in the justification for the responses.

By allowing students to work together on groupworthy tasks, teachers give students opportunities to develop academic language. From chapter 1, recall that the IRE (initiation–response–evaluation) instructional format allows only one turn of talk from one student to respond to a known-answer question. This format does not give students opportunities to develop verbal fluency in academic language or cultivate mathematical habits of mind. When concepts are developed in small-group settings with richly represented problems, students can first engage with ideas by using local language. For instance, students might first observe an increasing linear function by noting, "Look! This is going up," or, even further from academic language but with just as much intuition, they might slant their arm at an angle and say, "It goes like this." Their descriptions can get progressively more technical as students first interact with each other. One might ask, "How do you know it's going up?" and hear in response, "The *x* and *y* values are increasing." Later, with their teachers or the whole class, they can learn that this regular increase can be attributed to *slope*.

This layering in of representations, observations, and academic language supports all students' concept development, as the abstract terms emerge from observations they made in their own interactions. Mathematics educator Judit Moschkovich (1999) argues that developing ideas through representations is particularly important for English language learners, stating that diagrams, gestures, and graphs do more than provide extralinguistic cues; rather, they become a focus of meaning making for students.

Summary

In an equitable mathematics classroom, content needs to be reconceptualized in two important ways. First, mathematical knowledge includes more than just knowing *how* to do problems; it includes *how* and *why* certain approaches work and make sense. This conception not only moves school mathematics closer to the work of mathematicians, making it more rigorous, but also makes it more accessible. Justifications for why mathematics works give students an important entry point in mathematical thinking and help them understand and retain what they have learned.

This connection to student learning helps reconcile the seeming contradiction between making mathematics more rigorous and simultaneously accessible. In fact, in the past thirty years, substantial research has shown characteristics of robust mathematical thinking. If we want students to use their knowledge flexibly, they need to understand what they are learning. To help them understand, we must engage their prior conceptions. As has been suggested, mathematical thinking practices such as argumentation and justification support such understanding while encouraging students to view themselves as a source of mathematical knowledge. Finally, we are increasingly aware that students learn more than just content in school; they learn who they are in relationship to academic knowledge. Learning environments shape students' motivation, affect, and identities in ways that go beyond the traditional ideas about learning content.

Widely held assumptions about mathematics teaching do not hold true in a collaborative learning context. First, not only do teachers not need to start off with easy problems; starting with easy problems actually works against complex instruction. Challenging problems require greater interdependence than easy ones and send students the message that they can do difficult mathematics. Second, group work should not be viewed as an opportunity for smart students to teach struggling students. In a truly rich mathematical environment that supports multiple abilities, all learners help each other see problems from different perspectives.

For these ideas to be effective, students must be given mathematical problems that are groupworthy. That is, problems should (1) focus on central mathematical ideas, (2) be open-ended and incorporate multiple intellectual abilities, (3) have some aspect that is open to interpretation and offer multiple entry points into their solution, (4) work best when done in a group to bolster student interdependence, and (5) be designed and implemented to ensure both individual and group accountability.

Working with groupworthy problems can support the development of academic language, giving students vital opportunities to use mathematical terms and forms of talk while discussing ideas with their peers. This approach may particularly benefit English language learners, because the concepts can emerge from experiences with representations that can be accessed without heavy language demands. You can layer in increasingly complex academic language as students make observations about a problem together.

In this chapter, we focused on what an expanded view of mathematics that would incorporate mathematical thinking practices might look like and how those support students' engagement with challenging mathematical content. The example of the *Fractions or Not?* task illustrated some of those ideas in a familiar context. I talked about the group question routine as an important part of implementing the task in a groupworthy manner (fig. 4.3).

In the next chapter, I will elaborate on creating individual and group accountability systems in collaborative mathematical learning.

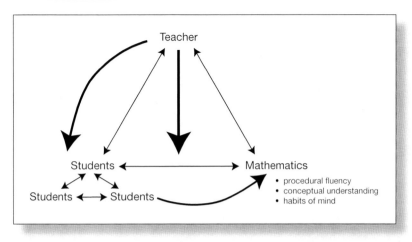

Fig. 4.3. Mathematics is broadened in the use of groupworthy tasks.

Fostering Positive Interdependence through Activities and Assessments

Group work involves more than students sitting around a table working on the same task. To reap the academic benefits of collaborative learning, students need to work together in ways that deepen everybody's understanding. For this reason, fostering *positive interdependence* is a primary goal for successful group work.

> *Positive interdependence arises when students feel mutual accountability for their learning and believe that their own learning will benefit through their interactions with each other.*

In earlier chapters, some of the strategies and concepts developed serve this purpose. In chapter 1, I talked about creating and maintaining *classroom norms* that support, among other things, students' sharing and use of each other's ideas. In chapter 2, I developed four principles for equitable teaching that guide teachers' understanding of the students in their classroom. In chapter 3, I built off these principles to challenge commonplace ideas about *smartness* and described how teachers can cultivate *equal-status interactions* in their classrooms by using *multiple-ability treatments* and *status interventions*. Students want to know what others think only if they believe that information will be useful. Traditional notions of smartness and common perceptions of status make it seem as if only certain people's thinking is worth engaging. In chapter 4, I discussed the kinds of activities that might be *groupworthy*—mathematics tasks that, among other things, create an authentic reason for students to solicit each other's thinking. Together, all these ideas and tools help teachers build learning environments that foster positive interdependence among students.

If interdependence is a value, teachers need to consistently communicate its worth through classroom norms, routines, and—most consequentially—assessments. In this chapter, I discuss aligning norms, routines, and assessments to the framework of equitable mathematics teaching in ways that support effective collaborative learning.

Norms and Routines

Norms to Support Positive Interdependence

As discussed in chapter 3, norms are a part of every classroom. Recall that classroom norms are agreed-upon ways of behaving. Here, I present some norms that apply specifically to collaborative learning and support positive interdependence (adapted from Cohen [1994]):

Stay focused on your group's work. No talking outside your group.
Students need to work only with the students in their assigned group. If students are not accustomed to working with any student in the class, they might try to communicate with friends in other groups or seek out answers from the "smart kids." Status plays into the desire to go outside the group, indicating that students do not believe that their group has the wherewithal to successfully do an activity together. By requiring students to work with the people at their table, teachers insist that every group has the capacity to make progress on the problem.

You have the right to ask anybody in your group for help.
Make explicit to students that they can ask anyone in their group for help. With this norm in place—and, ideally, visibly posted in the room—students who need help can appeal to the class rules if they are stuck. The next norm complements this one.

You have the duty to give help to anybody who asks.
Many students have learned that getting work done quickly is an effective way to do school. They are often reluctant to slow down and help a peer. They may feel that giving help interferes with their own learning, but on the contrary it often enhances it by presenting them an opportunity to make sense of their own thinking. In well-functioning collaborative classrooms, I hear teachers reminding students, "Use your group!"

Helping is not the same thing as telling.
Students often need guidance on what helping means. They must understand that they are teaching each other, not simply exchanging answers, which is a more common form of collaboration in school (see chapter 3's limited-exchange model). Two behavioral rules that might help support this particular norm are (1) "you can write only on your own paper" and (2) "you can let people see your paper, but you cannot hand it over to somebody else."

During whole-class discussions, teachers model asking questions to make sense of another student's mathematical thinking and communicate to students that their small groups should imitate this behavior (for more on the relationship between small-group norms and whole-class discussion, see chapter 6). As discussed in chapter 1, having conversations with students about acceptable behavior is one way of working toward certain norms. If classroom routines and activities contradict these conversations, students will usually gravitate toward familiar behaviors. I will discuss the potential contradictions between spoken and enacted norms in the next section.

Analyzing Activities

Norms are often more powerfully enacted than stated, so classroom activities require careful scrutiny for their contribution to messages about acceptable behavior. Simply stating norms is usually not sufficient for making them a reality in your classroom learning environment. Aligning routines and activities to be consonant with norms for productive collaborative learning poses a deep and ongoing challenge for teachers. Many activities are so commonplace, we often do not realize the messages that they send to students about norms, smartness, status, and mathematics itself. Teachers who are figuring out how to implement effective group work in their math classrooms are often surprised at how much they need to question the purpose, meaning, and messages of the most basic activities of classroom teaching and learning.

For example, a teacher may be working toward a classroom norm that *thinking carefully about a problem is valuable*. An activity that involves a speed calculation competition may work against this norm because it sends a strong (and familiar) message that quick computation is the primary way of being smart in mathematics. In fact, any competition runs the risk of reestablishing existing status hierarchies. (Some children, of course, enjoy competition. You can frame competitions to highlight their place and keep them from defining students' mathematical ability. For example, competitions on Pi Day [March 14] in which students see who can recite the most digits of π can be fun if they are communicated as one of many ways of being smart.)

Even if the teacher does not have official classroom competitions, students whose sense of smartness comes from their mathematical quickness might create a competitive environment through their actions. For instance, they might turn tests into races by loudly turning over their papers to signal to others that they have finished first. Such contests run counter to the equitable teaching principle that *all students can learn mathematics more deeply,* because this kind of activity may limit some students' opportunities to think carefully about what they are learning.

Students try to reconcile spoken messages about valuing different kinds of mathematical contributions with the experiences of competitive activities, regardless of whether the activities are official. Because children usually arrive in math class believing that speed competitions are not simply one but the *only* gauge of smartness, the hidden message of the activity often trumps the teacher's statement of what is valued. Teachers can explicitly praise when students take the time to be thoughtful and can request that students not make displays of their quick completion.

Consider another example of the need to closely align classroom activities with classroom norms. One teacher routinely gave unit test review packets that were similar to the actual test. Students would work together on them, but the focus of student conversations was on completion and learning the steps for doing each type of problem. The teacher realized that her students were not engaging deeply in the mathematics—her intended goal—as they worked through the review packets. The length of the packets pushed students to work through problems quickly and without seeking justification. They certainly were not distinguishing much between *helping* and *telling,* as she wanted them to do during collaborative work time; a limited-exchange model (chapter 3) was, in fact, the most efficient way to complete these assignments. The structure of making review packets similar to the tests encouraged students' strategy of memorizing for the assessment and forgetting soon afterward. In fact, for a student, this approach would be, in many ways, an optimal way to use the review packets. Thus, the activity worked against some of the sense-making and collaborative learning norms the teacher had sought to establish.

Mathematics activities may also depart from teachers' goals when they depend more heavily on nonmathematical skills such as reading comprehension or time management. Nonmathematical skills can overtake activities such as lengthy and complex word problems or long-term projects. This is not to say that teachers should never give tasks that demand such nonmathematical skills. In fact, for students to be prepared to use their mathematical skills in higher education or the workplace, requiring that secondary students do demanding and integrative tasks seems sensible. Nonetheless, teachers should recognize the nonmathematical aspects of activities and support students in ways that keep the content in the foreground. By attending to these parts of the task, teachers can minimize opportunity gaps that limit students' access to the mathematics.

For a general strategy, teachers can ask themselves the following questions to ensure that activities work in conjunction with equitable collaborative learning:

- What is the purpose of this activity?

- How does it align with my goals for the class?

- What kinds of mathematical smartness does this activity value?

- Do students have the skills and resources to engage in mathematics through this activity?

- Do other kinds of skills overshadow the mathematics?

- How does this activity align with the norms I have set up in my class?

- When students complete this activity, are my learning goals for them being met?

Teachers can use these questions to think through their classroom activities that may, like the unit test review packets, carry unwanted messages about mathematical learning.

Using Group Roles to Support Collaborative Norms

Two marks of productive group discussions are a creative interchange of ideas and well-distributed participation. These are signs of positive interdependence. Students must be taught ways of interacting that support this ideal. The norms discussed in the previous section help lead students in this direction.

Recall a central dilemma of group work: groups need autonomy for sense making, whereas teachers need assurance that important content is the focal point of discussion. Teachers resolve this dilemma by finding ways to delegate their authority by means of classroom structures. *Roles* are one such structure. Roles may be awkward for teachers initially. They often remark that telling students what to do in an activity feels artificial. This approach works best if, instead of thinking of roles as an impediment to spontaneous conversation, teachers conceptualize them as a tool for teaching students about desired forms of exchange and a means for ensuring distributed participation.

Although many different types of roles are possible, I offer here the four that I have seen work well in mathematics classrooms. When crafting roles for students, make sure that the roles are what Elizabeth Cohen referred to as *how* roles, not *what* roles. That is, the roles should relate to how the work is done (e.g., facilitator), not the parts of the tasks themselves (e.g., grapher).

The four roles are the following (source: Phil Tucher, Ruth Tsu, Barbara Shreve, and Carlos Cabana):

1. Facilitator

- Gets the team off to a quick start
- Makes sure everybody understands the task
- Organizes the team so they can complete the task

2. Resource monitor

- Collects supplies for the team
- Calls the teacher over for a question
- Cares for and returns supplies
- Organizes cleanup

3. Recorder/reporter

- Gives updates on the team's progress
- Makes sure each member of the team records work or data
- Organizes and introduces a group report

4. Team captain

- Encourages participation
- Enforces the use of norms
- Finds compromises
- Substitutes for roles if anybody is absent

Roles delegate teacher authority by distributing participation, giving each student something to do in the activity. In typical classrooms governed by the IRE talk format (initiation–response–evaluation; see chapter 1), teachers control the flow and content of conversation by taking ⅔ of the turns. In a collaborative learning environment, students manage important instructional conversations. Because group work is a large investment of class time, teachers need a say in the conduct of these conversations. Teachers do not abandon their authority; rather, it is decentralized and put toward fostering students' interdependence and autonomy.

When assigning roles, teachers should make them public so that everybody recognizes students' authority within their roles. The chart in figure 3.1 is a good way to publicly display group roles. Other teachers tape playing cards on the four corners of each group's shared table. For instance, one group might be "the jacks" and have the jack of hearts, spades, clubs, and diamonds on their desks. Each suit can represent one of four roles (e.g., the jack and 10 of hearts are the resource managers in their respective groups). This system makes apparent to everybody around the table which role each student is meant to play.

In addition to making roles public, teachers need to specify the expectations of people in each role, both in general and, on occasion, within a particular activity. The general expectations can be posted in the classroom, with the preceding text of the role descriptions. For a given activity, the specific role expectation can be written on a task card. (See chapter 4 for more on the design of task cards.)

Teachers are often inclined to assign leadership roles to students who are viewed as natural leaders. From a classroom management perspective, this approach is sensible, because it takes advantage of existing resources in the classroom. From a perspective of status, however, this approach is problematic because it reinforces existing hierarchies and does not give other students opportunities to develop leadership skills and contribute to collective thinking. With an eye toward equitable learning, teachers should give every child a chance to try all the roles. Doing so affords opportunities for students to increase their participation and learning while also raising their status, particularly if teachers are careful to ensure that the students assigned a role are also the ones to carry it out. A common status problem is for a higher-status student to take over a higher-status role.

Just as norms cannot be implemented by teachers' decree, roles also take some time and consistency to become effective. Students need to be taught to use roles well. In addition to clarifying expectations for the roles, teachers should supply explicit criteria for good group discussions. Not surprisingly, these line up with the norms for effective collaborative learning. As discussed earlier, three important norms are as follows:

1. Everyone gets a turn.

2. Give reasons for ideas.

3. Listen to different ideas.

We now add to that list a new norm. A key to fostering positive interdependence is giving each student something meaningful to do during collaborative work time: *Remember to play your role*. As teachers circulate around the classroom during collaborative learning time, they can remind students of these expectations.

Classroom Routines

Routines help the functioning of a classroom by giving students a predictable template for activities. Effective routines contribute to the functioning of the classroom by offering an efficient way to get things done. Students know the how, when, and where of things without having to ask. Routines also communicate norms and should be scrutinized for the messages that they communicate.

Most teachers have routines for turning in homework or taking tests. Students come to know the script for these activities and eventually can proceed with little need for explanation. Teachers can also create *interactional routines*—that is, routines that support positive interdependence among students. In chapter 4, I described the *group question* routine, in which teachers accept a question from the group only if the students have ensured that they have asked each other first. In addition to the described routine, note that only the *resource monitor* may ask the teacher to come over in the first place. This routine takes deliberate effort for both teachers and students to establish, because teachers tend to be inclined to answer any question posed to them. The payoff in fostering interdependence among students makes it a worthwhile endeavor, however, and that is one of the first routines teachers should invest themselves in.

Another important routine is called *quick start*. In this routine, students are expected to get themselves ready to work at the start of class. Their backpacks and materials should be in the expected place, out of the way. They should be at their desks or tables. The teacher should have an established way for class to begin, and students should get right to work. Teachers can make these expectations explicit and keep the structure the same so that students enter the room ready to work.

Some students have a difficult time starting an activity with their groupmates. Such students need time to process a task themselves before they start a discussion. Incorporating an *individual think time* routine might be wise. That is, when groups begin a task, tell facilitators to have the group take two minutes of quiet time to make their own notes before the groups' discussion begins. Alternatively, students can be asked to do a *quick-write activity* about their own thinking before they share with the group. For individual think time or quick-write routines to be effective, the activity must truly be groupworthy in that it requires multiple perspectives. If an individual student can complete the problem in that brief time, status problems will only be exacerbated.

Sentence starters can help students find the language for discussing their thinking together. If students have not had much experience in collaborative learning, they might have a hard time meeting norms such as *helping is not the same as telling;* they might know only how to tell. Teachers can post sentence starters in their classroom. Students may use them in a playful, singsong way at first. As they recognize their value, they can become natural ways for students to speak to one another.

Some good sentence starters include the following:

- *"How did you know how to* _____ *?"*
- *"What does* _____ *mean?"*
- *"* _____ *because* _____ *."*
- *"Why did you* _____ *?"*
- *"Why are our* _____ *different?"*

These sentence starters embody a strong push toward justification. The goal of sentence starters is to give students a way to have deeper mathematical conversations. In a limited-exchange format, students are used to asking each other, "What number are you on?" or "What did you get for problem 3?" These sentence starters help communicate different expectations and set them toward more creative interchanges. Likewise, sentence starters offer teachers a tool to support students in this work.

I will discuss other routines below, because they contribute to the accountability system in the classroom.

> "I think I figured out the importance of holding groups accountable for each other's understanding. When I consistently hold kids accountable for each other, I find understanding becomes more important then completion or product—which is what I wanted!"
>
> —*Laura Evans, Complex Instruction Educator, Mathematics Teacher, and Coach*

Accountability

Collaborative learning environments move important instructional conversations from the direct control of the teacher into students' control. Sometimes this approach is described as making learning environments that are *student centered* instead of *teacher centered*. Although this may be true in the context of who gets to speak, teachers must delegate their authority into students' conversations to ensure that they are mathematically meaningful. Ultimately, teachers want to support students in developing their own sense of mathematical authority through productive mathematical conversations—that is, by changing their thinking on the basis of the reasonableness of what is being argued. Norms and roles are two ways to accomplish this. Another way is through *account-ability*, both through informal routines during class time and through formal assessments.

Accountability through interactional routines

To support students' development of collaborative learning skills, teachers need to circulate around the room to enforce norms. The trick is figuring out when to intervene and when to stand back. Elizabeth Cohen's research on complex instruction has shown that hovering works against positive interdependence. Instead, she recommends that teachers intervene only in the following circumstances:

- When a group is hopelessly off task
- When a group cannot get started
- When a sharp interpersonal conflict arises
- When a group is falling apart because of a lack of organization

Even in these circumstances, teachers should usually take a moment before stepping in. Some teachers find it useful to take a few minutes to stand to the side of the room and take note of the range of what student groups are doing. (This chapter emphasizes the teacher's cultivation of group work norms. For more on the teacher's attention to the mathematics, see chapter 6.) They are often surprised at how much groups can function autonomously.

Nonetheless, interventions are sometimes needed. With an eye toward creating interdependence, teachers should be thoughtful about how they intervene. A good strategy is to stand close enough to listen and develop a sense of the underlying trouble before acting. Some questions to ask are the following:

- Is the task too hard?
- Is the mathematics bringing up status issues?
- Is one student resisting the authority or ideas of another?
- Are the students soliciting each other's ideas and listening to each other?
- Are the students distracted by a piece of juicy gossip or upcoming social event?

Once you have developed a hypothesis about the problem, choose your intervention accordingly.

Here are some examples of interventions in group work that hold students accountable to class norms (source: Phil Tucher, Ruth Tsu, Barbara Shreve, and Carlos Cabana):

- *Through an individual student, emphasizing the group role.* In this intervention, teachers direct a question or assign a task to a student in the context of a certain role. This approach helps bring the students back to the task and pushes that student to participate in the group conversation. For example, a teacher might say, "Who is the facilitator here? I want to see you keeping everybody together. It seems like we're having a hard time focusing today, so your team really needs you to do your job."

- *Through an individual student, regardless of group role.* This intervention method differs from the previous intervention by emphasizing a learning agenda that a teacher and student may have already discussed one on one. For instance, a teacher may be working with a student on getting her questions answered. A quiet aside to that student to see how it is going might support more effective collaborative learning.

- *To a small group.* As teachers circulate and listen in on conversations, they may have key questions prepared ahead of time that focus students on the vital conceptual issues of the task. (Chapter 6 will discuss these more.) Teachers should interrupt teams only as needed.

- *With the whole class.* Sometimes, as teachers go around the room, they see a common problem with either the process or the content of the group conversations. For instance, teachers may need to clarify the expectations of the task or remind students about the qualities of good conversations. Teachers should be mindful not to take away the mathematical heart of the task in this type of intervention.

- *Through a huddle.* An alternative strategy to address widespread difficulty is to call a huddle of all the students in the classroom who are playing the same role—for example, asking all resource monitors to come up to the front of the room. In the huddle, teachers might clarify directions, remind students of norms, check on work in progress, or ask students to share their groups' strategies. Huddles should be brief and have a clear purpose for what each student will bring back to his or her team.

- *Documenting for later.* A teacher may recognize a problem but choose to see how it plays out. This approach allows teachers to see how groups might recover from problems on their own. It may offer the basis for conversations with individual students or groups after class.

Two overarching priorities should shape teachers' interventions. First, the conversation should stay focused on students' mathematical learning. For instance, instead of scolding students for being distracted, a teacher might say, "I know you are excited about the dance tonight, but this is your chance to learn some important ideas about exponential functions. I want you to make the most of it." The second priority is to continue to push for positive interdependence. Students new to collaborative learning will often resist talking to each other and act upset that the teacher is not answering their questions as expected.

Conflicts

Although positive interdependence is a goal for effective group work, interpersonal conflicts will inevitably arise at some point. Teachers can choose whether to take arguing students aside or keep them within the small-group setting as a way of modeling conflict resolution. If the conflict continues and blocks productive learning, a teacher can publicly state, "It seems as if you two are having a hard time working together right now. I am going to switch you to other groups in the hopes that you will learn better somewhere else." Again, the focus in that statement remains on learning. Regrouping should be a last resort, because it works against the norm that everybody should be able to learn from anybody else in the classroom.

Students do not always know how to share their ideas with each other. A teacher sometimes needs to redirect students by creating experiences of positive interdependence by facilitating a conversation between students, as in the following example. As always, take some time to work out your solution to the problem so that you can follow the students' conversation.

Vignette 4: Working toward Positive Interdependence by Scaffolding Student Conversation

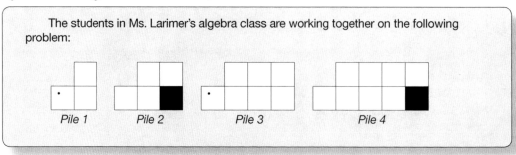

The students in Ms. Larimer's algebra class are working together on the following problem:

Pile 1   Pile 2   Pile 3   Pile 4

1. Sketch pile 5 and pile 6.

2. Use words to describe how pile 100 would look. Be specific.

3. Fill in the t-table.

Pile #	Perimeter	Area
0		
1		
2		
3		

*4. Find rules for the **perimeter** and **area** of each pile.*

In one group, Emory, Raúl, and Stefan work together. Emory calls Ms. Larimer over to her group. "Is this a group question?" Ms. Larimer asks. "Yes," says Emory. "We don't get how zero is supposed to work. My rule messes everything up."

Ms. Larimer kneels down next to the group and looks at Emory's paper. She asks, "What rule have you come up with?" Stefan holds up his paper and shows her his formula for the area, explaining, "Times 2, plus 1." Ms. Larimer repeats, "Times 2, plus 1." She notices that Emory's paper doesn't have the formula on it. Emory continues with her original question, "Zero messes it up."

Ms. Larimer asks, "Well, let's look at Stefan's rule. What's $0 \times 2 + 1$?"

Emory replies, using her method, "We can't find it because we don't know the perimeter. You take away 5 from the perimeter."

The teacher puts the students' papers side by side, and she sees that the students do not realize that they are using different approaches.

Pointing at the paper, she says, "Your rule looks different from Stefan's rule." She turns to Stefan. "Emory is saying that you have to know the area before you can find the perimeter?"

Emory answers, "Mm-hmm."

"Can you find a rule that doesn't rely on the area?"

Emory persists with the original question. "But if I look at the pattern, I don't get it. The perimeter equals 6 in the pattern and the area equals 1. So then, how would the shape look?"

Ms. Larimer says, "Good question." She turns to the boys. "What do you think?" She looks at Raúl, who has stayed quiet so far. Ms. Larimer asks, "Did you hear Emory's question, Raúl?"

Raúl responds, "No."

Ms. Larimer restates, "She wants to know what pile 0 is going to look like."

Raúl points to the numbers under the area column and says, "It goes like this: 14, 12, 10, 8, 6." He has yet another way of looking at the patterns.

The teacher responds, "What *rule* is that?"

Raúl answers, "The perimeter."

Ms. Larimer: "So, Raúl sees a pattern. Emory has a rule. And Stefan has a different rule." Stefan nods. Ms. Larimer turns to Stefan and says, "You three need to show each other how you are thinking about this. Put your work in the center of the table and explain it to each other. You won't be able to answer Emory's question until you hear each other's thinking." Stefan pushes his paper to the center of the table.

Ms. Larimer says, "I want you all to come together and I want you to discuss the patterns and formulas you have. It will help you figure out this perimeter issue. I'll come back and check with you in a bit."

Ms. Larimer looks at the students' mathematical work and makes a judgment that this group is not discussing their thinking. She interprets the mathematics and then decides how to intervene. Specifically, she facilitates students looking at and listening to each other's thinking. Mathematically, the students need to recognize that they are using three different methods that they have not yet reconciled. Stefan has come up with the formula $area = n \times 2 + 1$, where n equals the pile number. Emory is working with an implicit formula that $perimeter - 5 = area$. Raúl is working directly from the pattern emerging from the table. Emory's observation can help Stefan translate his area formula into a perimeter formula. Raúl's pattern can help them push on to the puzzle of pile 0. To interpret this challenging question, they need to understand the different ways of looking at the pile pattern and the connections among them.

Although Emory tells her that their question is a group question, they do not seem to have discussed their ideas in depth. They have different formulas on their papers and do not seem to recognize the differences. Ms. Larimer involves the students in each other's thinking in several ways. First, she puts the papers together and points out the different formulations, modeling the expectation that they should be closely comparing their work to come to shared understanding. Then, she communicates the expectation that they listen to each other when she asks Raúl, "Did you hear Emory's question?" She also rephrases some of their talk ("Emory is saying . . ."). Her work sets them up to listen to each other and make a productive mathematical comparison of their different approaches. Then she walks away so that she can support their productive interdependence.

Accountability through formal assessments
Why focus on assessment? Assessment is one of the most powerful ways teachers communicate their values to students. Secondary students are usually very attuned to "what counts" in a class, as is echoed in the common refrain, "Is this going to be on the test?"

Overwhelming research evidence shows that assessment plays an important role in classroom learning environments. We find three main problems in typical assessment approaches. First, assessment as usual does not promote good learning habits. Second, grading practices tend to emphasize competition over student learning. Finally, the feedback teachers give often has a negative effect, especially on low-achieving students, who see it as confirmation of their lack of ability (Black et al. 2004). For these reasons, if we want to design productive environments that support all students' mathematical learning, assessment plays a crucial role.

Just as equitable collaborative learning has required shifts in our views of teaching, mathematics, and student ability, it also requires a shift in thinking about assessment. Classroom assessment practices need to correct these negative outcomes and work toward learning and supporting student progress, no matter what their beginning level of achievement. Paul Black and Dylan Wiliam and their colleagues refer to this as *assessment for learning*, which they define as follows:

> An assessment for learning describes any assessment for which the first priority in its design and practice is to serve the purpose of promoting students' learning. It thus differs from assessment designed primarily to serve the purposes of accountability, or of ranking, or of certifying competence. An assessment activity can help learning if it provides information that teachers and their students can use as feedback in assessing themselves and one another and in modifying the teaching and learning activities in which they are engaged. Such assessment becomes "formative assessment" when the evidence is actually used to adapt the teaching work to meet learning needs. (Black et al. 2004, p. 10)

Assessments for learning are consonant with the four principles for equitable mathematics teaching introduced earlier in this book. First, by emphasizing learning, they distinguish learning and achievement. Second, by becoming a part of the feedback teachers use in their instructional design, these forms of assessment do not punish students for having missed opportunities to learn. Third, the focus on learning over summative evaluation pushes all students to learn mathematics more deeply. Finally, assessments for learning give students a role in classroom design when teachers adapt lessons to students' learning needs. Likewise, opportunities for self-assessment give students the chance to participate in the evaluation of their own learning. Although many forms of assessment for learning would engender positive and equitable learning environments, I focus in this chapter on the forms that support collaboration. Of course, individual student assessments are vital for accounting for each student's learning in addition to the group assessments described here.

What should teachers assess? What is worth assessing? Certainly the important ideas with which we want students to become fluent. In chapter 6, I discuss in more detail the key ideas that you want students to understand in a given activity. For now, I will focus on seven forms of assessment that help develop collaborative skills while deepening comprehension.

Self-evaluation. Teachers can periodically have students do a self-evaluation check of their group work skills. This can be a list of statements about group work norms with a rating scale of 1 to 5. For example, students can evaluate themselves on statements such as "I am patient with my teammates" and "I ask for help when I have questions." Students can also evaluate their adaptation to the learning environment, ranking themselves on statements such as "I know how to ask questions when I am confused." These self-evaluation documents can be an important resource for student or parent conferences. They can also offer a starting point for one-on-one conversations and give teachers a record of students' progress.

Checkpoints. Teachers may include explicit checkpoints in task cards (see chapter 4). A checkpoint requires the group to check their understanding of or progress on an activity before they move on to the next part. To prepare for checkpoints, teachers should have a few formative assessment questions ready. Students can proceed only if anybody, selected at random with a die, spinner, or other method, is prepared to answer a key question about the activity. When students know that any one of them can be accountable, they are more motivated to ensure one another's understanding.

Checkpoints foster interdependence by not letting anybody race ahead and raising the stakes for students to seek and offer help. Also, on longer tasks, checkpoints structure students' time by making a clear point for a teacher to check the content of their problem solving, so that students do not spend an entire class period working on an unproductive solution.

Shuffle quizzes. Shuffle quizzes give teachers a way of checking student work at the end of a task. Students are expected to keep their own written record of the work, and they know in advance that a shuffle quiz will be forthcoming, as the evaluation criteria state.

As with checkpoints, a teacher prepares for a shuffle quiz with a few formative assessment questions that will give a sense of students' understanding. The routine for a shuffle quiz involves the teacher coming over to a group who says that it has finished and every group member understands the solution. The teacher then collects the members' papers and holds them behind her back. After shuffling them around, she selects one at random. The student whose paper is chosen gets to answer the question. If that student does not answer the question satisfactorily, the students must work together to make sure that everybody understands the task deeply enough to succeed on another round of shuffling and questioning. The teacher reshuffles the papers for each question.

As an assessment structure, shuffle quizzes encourage interdependence because the students know that any one of them has to succeed at answering the teacher's question in order for the group work to be considered complete. They all know that they will be accountable for understanding the task deeply.

Group presentations. Students can organize a presentation of their thinking as a final product. Teachers can let students know ahead of time to prepare to do this. As we will discuss further in chapter 6, it may work for all students to prepare presentations and the teacher may select only some groups to actually present their thinking. Often, knowing that the possibility of a presentation exists is enough to encourage students to clarify their thinking.

If teachers are going to grade presentations, all groups will need a chance to present. Students should know ahead of time the criteria that the teacher will be grading them on. Do they need to explain their group's thinking? Do they need to explain how they may have gotten stuck? Also, a teacher who is going to ask a probing question about their solution should tell students that their grade will depend on *any* student in the group's ability to answer that question. This situation pushes students to confirm their groupmates' understandings of the solution.

Group posters. Group posters can be a part of group presentations or a separate product to be evaluated by teachers. In the former case, part of what groups present is an organized representation of their problem solving. Group posters can be a good way to organize group activity and compare across solutions. They are usually good as multiday activities and take a lot of class time and planning on the part of the teacher and students.

Sometimes, teachers might choose to have students create a poster, then using the posters as the basis for the group's grade. In that case, teachers need to communicate a grading scheme that includes clear evaluation criteria. Some assurance that all students have contributed to the poster also needs to be evident. Students can label the section of the poster that they helped with. Alternatively, teachers can let the groups know that, although they will not be doing a whole-class presentation, any group member should be prepared to answer a question about the mathematics in the poster. This question is a part of how the group's grade will be assigned. As with the group presentation, this accountability structure pushes students to confirm their groupmates' understandings of the mathematics.

Participation quizzes. Sometimes, teachers may recognize that a class needs to work on a few norms that would make their collaborative learning more productive. Here they may assign a participation quiz. The task for a participation quiz looks like any other groupworthy activity. The difference is that the teacher calls the students' attention to two or three group norms. For instance, the teacher might say, "Today, I really want to work on *playing your role* and *explaining your reasoning.* As you work, I will be listening for examples of people who are playing their role and giving reasons for their thinking." The teacher would then review each role and set the students to work. As the students work, the teacher publicly records each group's progress on working toward these norms. This might be done on an overhead, whiteboard, or butcher paper. It might look something like figure 5.1.

Participation Quiz	
Group 1: • + Got off to a quick start • + Facilitator: "Does everybody have his or her paper out?"	*Group 2:* • – Talking outside the group • + RM gets materials right away
Group 3: • + TC: "Does everybody understand what we are doing?" • – F works ahead of the group	*Group 4:* • + "Why did you put the 5 there?" • + TC keeping everyone together. • – F head on the desk
Group 5: • + "I don't get it. Explain how you did that." • + RM: "It has to be a group question."	*Group 6:* • – Talking outside the group • + TC: "No talking outside the group!"

Fig. 5.1. Notes a teacher might take during a participation quiz. Note the signs to let students know which behaviors are desirable (+) or undesirable (–). RM, resource monitor; TC, team captain; F, facilitator; R/R, recorder/reporter.

In the end, teachers can reflect on the students' work toward those norms in a public summary. The teacher who took the notes in figure 5.1 (which would be partial notes from a class session; a full set of notes would have much more content) might say, "I saw some of you really using your roles effectively" and point out specific examples. For some students, the public nature of this exercise is enough incentive to improve their adherence to classroom norms. For other classes, teachers may need to develop a scheme for assigning groups participation grades on the basis of the notes taken during class.

Group quizzes. Teachers sometimes feel a dilemma about test preparation. They want students to succeed, so they resort to giving students reviews that are similar to the actual test. Unfortunately, this tactic helps students learn only how to succeed on the test and often bypasses learning mathematics.

Group quizzes are an alternative to test reviews. Group quizzes should be organized like groupworthy tasks so that the structure is familiar to students. However, because they are a test, they differ in several ways.

First, they contain two to four big problems that encompass the major ideas of the unit of instruction. These problems are harder than problems that would appear on an individual test, because students have each other as a resource.

Second, the teacher explicitly does not answer questions because this is an opportunity for students to use what they know. To mitigate this factor, teachers might offer each group one hint during the group test. This approach supports groups' persistence in the face of challenging problems.

Third, the norm of not talking outside your group becomes essential during a group test.

Finally, teachers may decide to grade students on the work that they produce plus the quality of their conversations, taking notes similar to the ones that would be taken for a participation quiz. The goal of this activity is to push all students to think more deeply about the content as they review for an individual test. Group quizzes are generally designed to yield a group grade. Teachers may approach this by letting students know that they will randomly pick one paper to grade for each problem. This arrangement pushes students to check in with each other's work and make sure that all written work is of high quality. (The Annenberg Video Collection includes one called *Group Test,* showing students working on this kind of activity, along with interviews with the teacher about how he designed the task with his mathematical and learning goals for his students in mind, how he selected the problems, and productive ways to help students think them through. See *Teaching Math: A Grade 9–12 Video Library,* the Annenberg Foundation [1996], at http://www.learner.org/resources/series34.html.)

Summary

To support equal-status interactions and deep mathematical conversations, teachers need strategies for cultivating positive interdependence among students. Three main tools for this are the use of norms, routines, and, most consequentially, classroom assessments.

As discussed in chapter 3, norms are agreed-upon ways of doing things in a situation or setting. Specific norms foster positive interdependence, such as talking only within a group and asking only group questions. Norms are supported directly by classroom routines. Routines offer templates for activity that allow for predictability and hold students to set expectations. Several routines can also serve as interventions for when group work goes awry and help students build their collaboration skills.

Assessment plays a huge role in a classroom learning environment. Educational research has shown overwhelmingly that *assessment for learning* fosters more positive outcomes for students. In this chapter, we discussed several informal and formal accountability strategies, including student self-evaluation, checkpoints, shuffle quizzes, group presentations, group posters, participation quizzes, and group quizzes. These assessment tools may be unfamiliar to many teachers but can work to support classroom norms and routines and deepen students' positive interdependence.

In the next chapter, I will start to put together some of these components of supporting equitable collaborative learning by focusing on the teacher's role before, during, and after instruction.

Designing for Group Work:
The Teacher's Role
Before, During, and After Instruction

In the first five chapters, I introduced several important concepts and tools to support equitable group work. Here I offer teachers some guidance about planning successful group work lessons. I start by offering strategies for identifying worthwhile mathematical ideas. I then talk about ways of enhancing or adapting existing curriculum to make groupworthy tasks. I discuss how to start a group lesson, which differs from traditional problem launches by attending to multiple abilities and group roles. Next, using ideas from Margaret Smith and colleagues' (2008) *Thinking Through a Lesson Protocol* (TTLP), I discuss how to allot attention to different instructional goals, identifying what to listen for when monitoring small-group interaction. A vignette showing productive collaborative mathematical talk illustrates this concept. I consider how to organize time within the lesson to maintain cognitive demand. I end by discussing how teachers can use what they learned during the lesson about students' mathematical thinking and collaborative learning skills to plan the next lesson.

The goal of this chapter is to help teachers prepare to teach rich, groupworthy tasks in a way that supports students' collaborative mathematical thinking during instruction. Several studies document the way cognitively demanding tasks become proceduralized, diminishing students' learning opportunities. In other words, teachers sometimes succumb to the temptation to relieve students of their confusion and turn a complex task into a routine one.

Cognitively demanding tasks, of which groupworthy tasks are a subset, require students to do more than just apply previously learned procedures. Such tasks require high-level mathematical thinking, forcing students to make connections to the underlying mathematical ideas and engaging students in disciplinary activities of explanation, justification, and generalization. Although tasks might be designed to be cognitively demanding, teachers can enact them in classrooms in low-level ways. This can happen when teachers take away the conceptual heart of the problem by suggesting an approach, giving students little to grapple with: the pedagogical equivalent of telling "whodunit." Sometimes, in response to confusion, teachers model a similar problem, in the mode of traditional instruction (chapter 1), leaving students the task of successfully imitating that solution.

Instead of avoiding confusion, teachers need to shift into helping students through their confusion. Doing so is the essence of maintaining cognitive demand. Mathematics educators Marjorie Henningsen and Mary Kay Stein (2002) have detailed some of the ways teachers maintain cognitive demand. First, teachers succeed in maintaining mathematical richness when the activity successfully builds on students' prior learning. Teachers need to think through their lessons to ensure that students are making adequate connections. At the same time, teachers must be cautious not to "overscaffold." Teacher support should help students engage their thinking, not do the thinking for them, through asking the kinds of questions described in chapter 4. Likewise, students need adequate time to make sense of the task. Rushing through almost necessitates that students bypass careful thinking. As described in chapters 4 and 5, students need to have a sense of the criteria on which the teacher will judge their performance. When teachers articulate what they are looking for, students have a better sense of what a good performance entails. Finally, cognitively demanding tasks maintain their power when teachers consistently press for meaning around students' activities. Classroom norms that demand that students justify their thinking help support this goal.

How do teachers plan lessons that meet all these criteria? Groupworthy tasks, by design, are open-ended and invite a variety of student interpretations. This variability creates greater uncertainty for teachers, because they no longer control classroom activity in the same way they do when teaching focuses mainly on clear presentation of ideas. The trade-off in student learning and participation is well worth it, but gaining facility in these methods takes some time. In addition to the group work structures described in earlier chapters, teachers can take specific actions to sustain the richness of mathematical tasks while keeping students engaged. The frameworks that I present here can guide teachers' activities during instruction, supporting high levels of student engagement and preparing for rich whole-class discussions, moving away from a show-and-tell approach to one focused on mathematical sense making.

In the rest of this chapter, I describe how teachers can help students sustain their engagement. Before anything else, teachers must shift how they view their curriculum, moving away from a view of mathematics as a sequence of topics to a web of connected ideas. I then outline work to do before, during, and after instruction that supports equitable collaborative learning.

Rethinking Curriculum:
Finding Worthwhile Mathematical Ideas

What is worth teaching? We have our students for a limited amount of time, and we want to make sure that the content we focus on will have the most payoff for their mathematical learning, now and in the future.

This question, posed by educators Grant Wiggins and Jay McTighe in their 2005 book *Understanding by Design*, is not a question mathematics teachers are accustomed to hearing. Most teachers have learned to follow a curricular sequence handed down through state standards documents or textbook materials. In keeping with the richer vision of mathematics that groupworthy tasks necessitate (chapter 4), teachers need to do more than follow a curricular sequence. To know what ideas to draw out and push on, they need to clarify for themselves and their students the important understandings about the topics at hand, even within a specified curricular framework.

Wiggins and McTighe suggest that teachers ask themselves the following questions about the content that they teach:

- What *understandings* about key ideas should students leave with?

- What *big ideas* should anchor and organize the content, framed as essential questions?

- What do *common misunderstandings* suggest the desired understandings ought to be?

- What should students leaving my classroom be able to do *on their own*?

The answers to these questions are not always obvious to secondary mathematics teachers. Think of a topic you teach, and try to answer these four questions in full sentences. In designing learning goals, moving away from the language of skills ("Students will calculate slopes") to the language of understanding ("Students will identify common features of linear growth and find slopes by using multiple mathematical representations") is often challenging.

Because teachers were typically taught mathematics in a topic-to-topic fashion, they tend to think of the subject as one of learning terms and practicing procedures (as described in chapter 1). Moving past thinking of mathematical learning as *moving through a sequence of topics* to *developing enduring understandings* challenges educators to rethink familiar content.

Obviously, to comprehensively revisit the entire secondary mathematics curriculum and push on these questions is beyond the scope of this book. Fortunately, good materials are available to help teachers explore the conceptual side of mathematics and develop their own answers. One rich resource comes from mathematics educator Mark Driscoll. Along with his colleagues at the Educational Development Center, he has developed frameworks for big ideas and essential questions in algebra and geometry (Driscoll 1999; Driscoll et al. 2007).

For example, a big idea in algebra is that *anything we do mathematically, we find a way to undo*. This idea supports more enduring understandings. Instead of students' learning algebra topics, we teach them to think algebraically, a useful skill in all walks of life. Algebraic thinking is useful in mathematics classrooms too, supporting students in making generalizations. For instance, students can understand equation solving beyond "doing steps" and see that equation solving, because of the ideas of doing and undoing, is possible because every operation in mathematics has an inverse. Using inverse operations is key to isolating variables when solving equations. Having a sense of this big idea helps teachers focus lessons, lets teachers tie seemingly different problems together, and allows students to predict what might be needed for an unknown problem, all of which contribute to deeper, more enduring understandings. (For more elementary topics, some good resources include Van de Walle et al. [2010] and Marilyn Burns' many excellent books [e.g., Burns 2007].)

Groupworthy problems should contribute to these deeper understandings and center on big ideas. Procedural topics are, of course, a part of any mathematics curriculum. When choosing which topics to invest with the time and effort of collaborative learning, teachers should focus on anchoring ideas that will be worth going back to throughout the unit of instruction and over the year.

Setting Up Your Classroom for Collaboration

What should the physical environment to support equitable collaborative learning look like? On the most basic level, teachers need desks that can move together or tables for students to sit at together. Ideally, tables should be on an equal plane so that students can easily share work. A group can have four to five students, and there should be an aisle for the teacher to circulate.

A hanging seating chart with students' names on cards signaling students' group assignment and their role also helps. Sometimes teachers label groups numerically, hanging numbered labels above the clusters of desks. This system allows students to know where to go without having to ask the teacher. Transparency of these structures supports the goal of student autonomy.

Around the room, teachers might post signs that they can discuss or simply gesture to as a way of communicating class expectations. Using text from this book, teachers can create signs with group role descriptions, lists of classroom norms, sentence starters, different mathematical smarts, and the word *YET* (see Inflated Talk about Self or Others in chapter 3). Likewise, some teachers find a representation of the learning process helps normalize confusion, as in figure 6.1. Teachers can introduce students to their expectations through these signs. Later, a wave of the hand toward a sign sometimes suffices to remind students about class norms.

Unless students have been working collaboratively in other classrooms, teachers will need to teach students

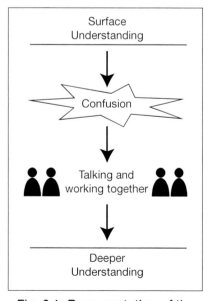

Fig. 6.1. Representation of the normal learning process to support students' progress

how to work together productively. The physical arrangement of the room, along with the accountability systems described in chapter 5, are important tools for teaching students how to learn together effectively.

Before Instruction: Thinking Through a Lesson

Margaret Smith and her colleagues have developed a protocol for what they describe as *Thinking Through a Lesson* (Smith, Victoria, and Hughes 2008). Because open-ended, cognitively demanding tasks necessarily require more input from students, the path through them is less evident to teachers at the outset. By thinking through the lesson, teachers can get a better handle on how students might respond to an activity and anticipate such responses in ways that support meaningful mathematical thinking.

The *Thinking Through a Lesson Protocol* (TTLP; fig. 6.2) asks teachers to work in three phases to go beyond simple lesson planning toward anticipating the kinds of mathematics students might develop in the context of a given task. The first part of TTLP focuses on *selecting and setting up the task*. This thinking stems from the kind of curricular perspective discussed in the previous section. Teachers need to identify their mathematical goals and connect these to students' prior

---

Part 1: Selecting and Setting Up a Mathematical Task

What are your mathematical goals for the lesson (i.e., what do you want students to know and understand about mathematics as a result of this lesson)?

In what ways does the task build on students' previous knowledge, life experiences, and culture? What definitions, concepts, or ideas do students need to know to begin to work on the task? What questions will you ask to help students access their prior knowledge and relevant life and cultural experiences?

What are all the ways the task can be solved?

- Which of these methods do you think your students will use?
- What misconceptions might students have?
- What errors might students make?

What particular challenges might the task present to struggling students or students who are English language learners? How will you address these challenges?

What are your expectations for students as they work on and complete this task?

- What resources or tools will students have to use in their work that will give them entry into, and help them reason through, the task?
- How will the students work—independently, in small groups, or in pairs—to explore this task? How long will they work individually or in small groups or pairs? Will students be partnered in a specific way? If so, in what way?
- How will students record and report their work?

How will you introduce students to the activity so as to provide access to *all* students while maintaining the cognitive demands of the task? How will you ensure that students understand the context of the problem? What will you hear that lets you know students understand what the task is asking them to do?

Fig. 6.2. Questions for teachers using the TTLP (adapted from Smith, Bill, and Hughes [2008])

Part 2: Supporting Students' Exploration of the Task

As students work independently or in small groups, what questions will you ask to

- help a group get started or make progress on the task?
- focus students' thinking on the key mathematical ideas in the task?
- assess students' understanding of key mathematical ideas, problem-solving strategies, or the representations?
- advance students' understanding of the mathematical ideas?
- encourage *all* students to share their thinking with others or to assess their understanding of their peers' ideas?

How will you ensure that students remain engaged in the task?

- What assistance will you give or what questions will you ask a student (or group) who becomes quickly frustrated and requests more direction and guidance in solving the task?
- What will you do if a student (or group) finishes the task almost immediately? How will you extend the task so as to provide additional challenge?
- What will you do if a student (or group) focuses on nonmathematical aspects of the activity (e.g., spends most of his or her [or their] time making a poster of their work)?

Part 3: Sharing and Discussing the Task

How will you orchestrate the class discussion so that you accomplish your mathematical goals?

- Which solution paths do you want to have shared during the class discussion? In what order will the solutions be presented? Why?
- In what ways will the order in which solutions are presented help develop students' understanding of the mathematical ideas that are the focus of your lesson?
- What specific questions will you ask so that students will
  1. make sense of the mathematical ideas that you want them to learn?
  2. expand on, debate, and question the solutions being shared?
  3. make connections among the different strategies that are presented?
  4. look for patterns?
  5. begin to form generalizations?

How will you ensure that, over time, *each* student has the opportunity to share his or her thinking and reasoning with peers?

What will you see or hear that lets you know that *all* students in the class understand the mathematical ideas that you intended for them to learn?

What will you do tomorrow that will build on this lesson?

Fig. 6.2. (continued)

learning experiences, both in and out of school. Teachers are also asked to anticipate the different ways students might solve the task, imagining both methods and potential misconceptions that might arise. Using the answers to these questions, teachers then consider the resources they might provide and how they might set up the task to support students' work.

Using the *Fractions or Not?* task (fig. 4.2) as an example, teachers might recognize that their goal is to get students to focus on the meaning of fractions and how fractions are represented. Teachers could anticipate that some students would be misled by the representations in diagrams

2 and 4 of figure 4.2, wanting to see the "whole" as either four pieces or nine pieces, because the arrangement and shape leads them in this direction. Teachers should also anticipate an important debate about diagram 3, as students deliberate over whether the square in the middle of the diagram is a hole or part of the whole.

In the second part of TTLP, teachers think through how they might *support students' exploration of the task*. Building from the thinking from the first part of TTLP, teachers can develop key questions that will get at critical ideas without proceduralizing student work. In the *Fractions or Not?* task, for example, a question that gets at the conceptual heart of the problem would be, "What is the part, and what is the whole?" Amid the confusion that diagrams 2, 3, and 4 could cause, this question would press students to articulate their assumptions and connect it to the targeted big idea about fractions.

In the third part of TTLP, teachers *anticipate different student strategies* and how they might want to select among them during the whole-class discussion. The goal is to bring out different ways of thinking about the problem, leveraging them to deepen students' shared understanding. If a teacher is using a task for the first time, proceeding with the third part of the TTLP without assistance from colleagues is often difficult (see chapter 7 for more about working with colleagues). Once teachers have used a task or if they have good resources to draw from, seeing in advance where the important discussion points might be becomes easier.

In addition to these concerns, teachers practicing complex instruction want to think about the multiple-ability orientation for their task. Looking at the activity and the anticipated strategies, what kind of mathematical competence do they draw on? This consideration should go into the multiple-ability orientation that teachers use at the beginning of the lesson. The list of abilities prepares teachers better to listen during class time and figure out the different ways that students are smart.

> "If you identify the multiple abilities in your tasks before class, you will surprise yourself with how much more you are able to assign competence during class—perhaps even every kid!"
>
> —*Nicole Bannister, Mathematics Teacher and Teacher Educator*

In *Fractions or Not?* a teacher might want to spend more or less time discussing diagram 1, depending on an assessment of the class's understanding of the importance of fractions coming out of the division of a whole into *equal* parts. The potentially different interpretations of diagram 3 would lead a teacher to allot sufficient time to arguments for viewing the center square as a part of the whole or as a hole, an issue that arises no matter the class's overall level of proficiency with fractions. Along with considering the mathematical content, teachers can think through their particular students and the participation goals for their classes. Whom do they need to hear from? Whose understandings are they concerned about? How can they develop group interdependence and leverage accountability to ensure good discussions at each table (see chapter 5)?

During Instruction: Monitoring, Selecting, Sequencing, and Connecting

Before instruction, students' work is a hypothetical built from teachers' previous experience with the content, students of that age group, and the particular personalities in the classroom. Sometimes, teachers are pleased with their ability to successfully anticipate students' responses, and lessons run relatively smoothly. Of course, no matter the level of teacher experience with the curriculum or age group, something unexpected may occur during students' mathematical explorations.

Beginning an Activity

Beginning an activity consists of an orientation phase, a multiple-ability treatment, and delegation of teacher authority.

Mathematical orientation

For a collaborative learning lesson, teachers start by discussing the mathematical issues that will be focused on today. To do so, teachers focus on the big ideas they have identified in their planning, using *inquiry* language. Inquiry language differs from *work completion* language; inquiry focuses on the mathematical issues in play. Instead of saying, "You will be doing Investigation 7" (work completion), teachers say, "Today, you will be thinking about the different relationships among angles formed by parallel lines with another line cutting through them" (inquiry).

Multiple-ability treatment

To set students up for positive interdependence, teachers then provide students with a multiple-ability treatment (see chapter 3). Such treatments let students know what mathematical abilities will help them succeed with the task. For example, in the *Fractions or Not?* task, students need to use complex visual reasoning, apply definitions, think systematically, and make good arguments. A multiple-ability treatment is followed by the message, "Let me remind you that no one of us has all of these abilities, but all of us have some of them. Use each other, and you can make progress on this task." The last statement creates a mixed set of expectations to help disrupt existing status hierarchies. These multiple-ability treatments play a crucial role in creating equal-status interactions (Cohen and Lotan 2003).

Delegating authority through the task card and group roles

When teaching centers on clear explanations and without productive collaboration, teachers are the main source of knowledge in the classroom. For these reasons, clear instructions at the start of a task are essential. In a collaborative setting, teachers delegate their authority more quickly. After the multiple-ability treatment, students can be told to get into their groups and the task card can be distributed.

The task card should contain enough information for students to begin their work on the problem. Instead of reading instructions to students, teachers delegate authority by explaining to students how they will get each other started on the task. For instance, a teacher might say, "When you get your task card, I want facilitators to make sure that the directions are read aloud. Team captains, after the directions are read, check in to make sure everybody understood. Recorder/reporters, make sure to have paper out so you are ready to write. Okay, resource monitors, come up and get the cards for your groups." In this way, two of the vital tools for the delegation of teacher authority are put to use: task cards and roles. The teacher has given each student something active to do in the launching of the task. All students need to participate.

The teacher's work then becomes about making sure that the students are doing their job to get each other started on the task. Only the resource monitors may call the teacher over, and then only if it is a group question. (See the group question routine, chapter 4.) This system takes considerable letting go on the part of the teacher, but teachers are often astonished at how much students can accomplish on their own.

During the Activity

As the students progress on the task, the teacher circulates around the room, listening but not hovering. The teacher pays attention to student thinking and group dynamics, intervening only occasionally (see chapter 5 regarding teacher hovering and when to intervene). Student autonomy is the goal. Teachers must shift from relieving students from their confusion to helping them through it. Teachers need to resist the temptation to proceduralize not only at the start of a task but also during it. If the students get frustrated, teachers can remind them that confusion is part of learning and will eventually help them deepen their understanding. They can then facilitate discussions and peer-to-peer listening to help students turn their conversations more productive for learning (see vignette 4 in chapter 5 for an illustration of scaffolding peer-to-peer listening). Some teachers find it helpful to purposefully stand to the side of the room for a few minutes at the start of a task, forcing the students to use each other.

What am I looking for?

Teachers want a sense of what productive group discussion might look like. When can they stay back and know that their authority has successfully been delegated? How do they know when they have managed to design for equal-status interactions? What does positive interdependence look like, exactly?

In its essence, productive small-group discourse should enable students to listen to each other's mathematical reasoning, pressing each student to deepen his or her understanding while considering different ways of interpreting a problem. Teachers should hear a lot of mathematical talk from a wide range of students. Students should press each other for justification, feel free to state their confusions, and reconcile their perspectives. Important content issues should surface.

The following vignette illustrates how students can work together to deepen their understanding of mathematics.

Vignette 5: Students Reconciling Different Equations to Deepen Algebraic Understanding

Sal, Keisha, Tanya, and Min are working on the following problem:

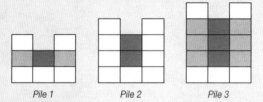

Pile 1   Pile 2   Pile 3

1. Sketch pile 4 and pile 5.
2. Use words to describe how pile 100 would look. Be specific.
3. Find a formula for the perimeter.
4. Describe pile 0.

The students are working on question 3 on the task. Min says, "I don't get it. How are we supposed to find the formula?" Tanya has started making a table with the pile numbers in the left-hand column. She starts counting the perimeters and filling the table in. She turns her paper to the group, "Like this, see?" Keisha looks at her paper and says, "Oooh! Yeah. Okay. Like that other one." The students work together to find the perimeters for piles 1–5, and Tanya, the group's recorder, writes them down:

1	14
2	16
3	18
4	20
5	22

Sal kneels in his chair to look across the table at Tanya's paper. "Okay! Wait, hang on." He writes on his paper intently. Meanwhile, Keisha picks up the task card and starts working on her paper at the same time.

Sal says, "I got it! 2*n* + 12. 'Cause, see, this goes up by 2"—he gestures down the right-hand column of the table—"14, 16, 18; it's plus 2. So that's the 2*n*. Then I just figured out the other part."

Keisha looks at her paper. "Nuh-uh. That's wrong. Look at the picture. It's 8 + (*p* + 2) × 2."

Min looks at Keisha's formula and frowns. "Oooh! That's ugly!"

Tanya looks baffled. "How'd you get that?"

Keisha says, "It's ugly, but it's right." She puts the task card in the middle of the table. "See? This and this is the same in all of them. It's always 8." She traces her finger along the top of each diagram, showing the constant perimeter of 8. "Eight, eight, eight. So that's that. And look, each side is 2 more than the pile number." She gestures at each pile, pointing to its number and its side, saying, "Dun, dun, dun, dun . . . So that's *p* plus 2 minus—"

Sal interjects, "I like *n* better than *p*."

Keisha looks annoyed and says, "Well, *p* makes more sense 'cause it's *piles*. But there's two sides each time, so that's *times* 2. Voilà." She leans back and smiles proudly.

Sal says, "Yeah, but it's still ugly. I like mine better. And I think I'm right. Look." Sal plugs each of the values in the table into his formula, triumphantly showing Keisha that his works.

"That's weird," says Tanya. She holds the papers side by side. After a pause, she says, "What if we multiply through on Keisha's?" She picks up her pencil and calculates. The students lean over and talk to her as she does the simplification out loud, helping her with the distribution calculation.

"Whoa! No way!" Tanya shouts. They are pleased to discover that the two answers are the same, smiling and doing little victory dances.

Discussion

In vignette 5, the students reconciled two seemingly different rules for the perimeter of the pile pattern. Sal built his rule from the table that Tanya generated, whereas Keisha worked from the diagram. Each representation yielded different, sensible formulas. Because the students were beginning their study of algebra, they did not initially recognize the equivalence of the expressions they generated. Once Tanya got the idea to make Keisha's rule "not ugly," they were delighted by the equivalence. The reconciliation created an engaging context to deepen their understanding of simplifying expressions. The way the two students generated their formulas yielded a potentially interesting discussion for the teacher to take up, because the difference illustrates algebraic relationships with distinctive representations. Sal's formula showed a relationship to the table, as the +2 increase in the ordered table of values showed up in the slope coefficient. Keisha's formula illustrated a relationship to the geometry of the diagram, with each number in the expression mapping onto the shape of the pile.

The discussion among the students illustrates several qualities of positive interdependence. Min, who comfortably declared her confusion early in the conversation, made positive contributions to the discussion. Although she participated differently, she was not left out. Tanya, in her role as recorder/reporter, took primary responsibility for generating the table that Sal used to build his formula. Keisha and Sal were generating formulas, but Tanya stayed in the conversation and had the key insight into how to reconcile the different expressions. The group engaged Keisha's formula, even though Sal was a higher-status student; one can easily imagine a classroom where the "ugly" formula is dismissed outright. She had the confidence in her thinking to stand up for her formula, even when the others teased her playfully about its appearance. Keisha's mathematical smartness here was in interpreting the visual representation algebraically. She had a harder time than Sal articulating her thinking, but the small-group setting allowed her to justify her reasoning by using picture and gestures, supporting effective communication.

Listening to Student Thinking

A common misconception exists that student-centered teaching focuses on student thinking so much that the discipline of mathematics disappears. This is wrong. Along with the management of student participation by using the structures of group work discussed in earlier chapters, teachers need to manage students' mathematical thinking during the class session and hold it accountable to the discipline. Although discussions like that among Min, Sal, Keisha, and Tanya are the goal, they do not typically come about without teacher support.

The four main activities teachers engage in during instruction are monitoring, selecting, sequencing, and connecting (Stein et al. 2008). Monitoring occurs during most of students' collaborative work time. Teachers monitor student work at two levels. First, to ensure high-quality collaborative talk, using the tools and frameworks discussed in previous chapters, teachers work as norm enforcers, reminding students to justify their thinking, to talk inside their group, to make sure everybody understands, and that any question they ask the teacher must be a group question. At the same time, teachers support productive mathematical engagement, building off students' thinking through the lesson and redirecting any negative behavior through a focus on learning goals.

Monitoring has two components. The mathematical part involves paying attention to the kinds of student thinking that happen during students' collaborative work time. This is, in its essence, a form of assessment for learning (chapter 5). Teachers also attend to the social aspects of class-work. Although the math or the social dynamics might be more in play, teachers do both simultaneously, answering student questions and keeping groups on task. Some like to prepare a checklist for collaborative learning time to monitor the group work behaviors they see, with space for notes about the content of different student solutions. Whatever method they use, teachers should be thinking about the kinds of learning opportunities that different mathematical methods could contribute to the whole class's understanding, paying attention to issues of representation, validity, and breadth of approaches, as well as airing common misconceptions. The most instructionally productive student work may not be the most elegant, as with Keisha's "ugly" formula. Students can learn a lot from unexpected formulations or a well-explained error as well as from a geometrically insightful "ugly" approach.

This step then leads to the task of *selecting* which solutions to present to the whole class. Two main strategies are part of selection: sharing group disagreements and sequencing solutions. If the teacher overheard the rich mathematics discussed in the previous vignette, the students might be asked to come and present their disagreement to the class so that others can comment on the mathematics the students developed. Students often find it engaging to weigh in on mathematical controversies, and different students' thinking can be layered into the original disagreement. In sequencing, teachers, as they monitor, note the different interpretations that students bring to a problem. The teacher then purposefully determines the order for presentations of student solutions. A common strategy is to begin with misconceptions. Of course, if this strategy is used all the time, students will become reluctant to be picked first, assuming that going first means that their solution is incorrect. Another approach is to get the answer out quickly so that the discussion's purpose is clearly how students thought about the problem rather than as a means for simply verifying the answer. (A good video example of this strategy in use comes from Cathy Humphrey's teaching, chapter 2 in Boaler and Humphreys [2005].)

When using groupworthy problems, a teacher can avoid status issues by having students share their different interpretations of the problem—as in the different possible formulas in the pile pattern problem or the different interpretations of the diagrams in the *Fractions or Not?* activity (fig. 4.2). Thus, the ordering does not focus on a hierarchy of misconceptions to correct conceptions; instead, it focuses on different ways of approaching a problem. Teachers must attend to issues of status when sequencing.

Purposeful sequencing can build contrasts that meet teachers' mathematical goals. In sequencing the *Fractions or Not?* discussion, a teacher might notice that most of her students saw the square in the middle of diagram 3 as a hole and counted the fraction as ¾. Here the teacher may have a student group present this solution first before moving on to the more subtle interpretation of the hole as being a part of the whole. A sequence of questions would help the first group of students make sense of the second solution. What is the whole in your view of this picture? What are the parts? Can you determine the fraction shown by the shaded area? How did you decide? We can imagine a similar list of questions for the pile pattern problem in vignette 5, highlighting the mathematical issues of the value of simplifying and how the structure of formulas maps onto different algebraic representations.

Norms are communicated during all classroom activities. When teachers are sequencing solutions, partial solutions are acceptable starting points for a whole-class discussion. This tactic communicates the valuation of mathematical thinking over hurried but complete work. If, during monitoring, teachers see similar solutions across the class, they may prioritize the social goals of teaching students how to share work publicly. That is, a teacher may select groups to present randomly, using a spinner or die, thus keeping students prepared to share their thinking. Random selection disrupts any patterned choices that may cause students to interpret status judgments in selection or nonselection decisions.

What if *all* students interpret a problem in the same way? Would the teacher lose the opportunity to bring up more mathematically interesting interpretations? Not necessarily. Teachers can introduce other approaches that illuminate important mathematical issues by referring to "another solution I've seen" or "what somebody did in another class" (Boaler and Humphreys 2005).

Comparing Solutions to Generalize, Justify, and Represent Mathematical Thinking

Once teachers decide how to sequence the solutions, they can identify their goals for the whole-class discussion of the solutions or approaches. Critical learning happens when students analyze different approaches or solutions. Teachers should support students' use of mathematical thinking practices, such as generalizing, justifying, and representing their thinking. Some prompts teachers might use for generalizing include questions such as the following:

- Can you give me the *rule*?
- Is it *always* true?
- Does it work *every* time?

Generalizing also grows from comparing solutions. For example, a student group might be asked to describe the difference between their solution and the one presented before theirs, with a question such as, "How is your graph different from that one?" Teachers can communicate the importance of generalization throughout the discussion by reminding students to look for patterns as solutions are presented. "Watch as we see the different solutions. Do you notice any patterns?"

Justifying is supported by questions that ask students to explain their reasoning. For example:

- Where did that number come from?
- Can you explain how you decided to use that strategy?

Teachers should press for justification during students' collaborative work time too, through norms such as "say your 'becauses.'" In this way, whole-class discussions and group work support the same norms.

Representing—depicting mathematical ideas, modeling situations with visual aids, or interpreting diagrams or pictures—is often a place where students learning English can participate more readily. Because drawing and gesturing can limit the need for language, some students can express their thinking more easily through representations. Some prompts for representing include the following:

- Draw what you just explained on the diagram.

- Which part of the graph tells you the solution?

- How did you see the pattern in those pictures?

Whole-class discussions should include all these mathematical thinking practices and a comparison of solutions to help students understand how different approaches compare. The issues of mathematical *equivalence* and *uniqueness* are at the heart of thoughtful comparisons.

Equivalence is recognizing what objects and operations are the same. The simplification of Keisha's geometrically derived equation revealed its equivalence to Sal's table-derived one. Equivalence is a mathematical issue that occurs throughout the curriculum. Understanding, for example, how 0.5, ½, and 50% can all represent the same proportion is an essential connection for student understanding. Likewise, when students can explain how a 180° rotation of an object in the plane can be reproduced by using reflections and translations, they have a better sense of the meaning of these transformations. Sometimes students' seemingly disparate solutions help reveal the underlying equivalence relationships between mathematical objects and processes.

On the other side of equivalence is uniqueness. Many students enjoy that mathematics, unlike other subjects, has answers rooted in logic. Knowing when solutions are unique is also of interest and worth investigating. When they come upon an interesting pattern, they can probe it by asking whether it is always true. Doing so pushes the need to develop careful generalizations. These questions of equivalence and uniqueness can be engaged in a productive comparison of student solutions.

Using Whole-Class Discussion to Support the Norms of Collaborative Learning

By designing whole-class discussions in this way, teachers can support the norms and expectations for productive group work. They can use the same sentence starters that they expect students to use during their discussions. They can model the kinds of sense-making questions they expect to see students asking each other during presentations. Most important, they can make the expected relationship between the whole-class talk and the small-group talk transparent by interjecting, "Do you hear the explanation Marcus gave? That was so clear. He told us how he was thinking by using lots of 'becauses.' I want to hear you doing that when you work together too." This is also an opportunity to assign competence to Marcus for justifying his solution. Issues of status are in play in the whole-group setting as well, and teachers can find ways to attend to and address them during these discussions.

Because whole-class discussions are another activity in a classroom learning environment, they should communicate values and expectations that align with the ones established for small-group work.

Figure 6.3 gives a template for lesson planning across a TTLP and a complex instruction framework.

After Instruction:
Reflecting and Responding to Build the Next Lesson

When teachers let students talk about their mathematical thinking and provide structures to engage students' ideas, they are often surprised at how much they see familiar content with new eyes. This process often pushes teachers to rethink their own understanding of mathematics. Bringing the social dimensions of the classroom in the mix—norms, status, and participation patterns—teachers

Orientation: Emphasize the Groupworthiness of the Task	
Content and task directions • What minimal content overview is needed to provide access and context to the task? • What minimal task directions are needed? What kind of task card? What oral instructions?	Roles • What roles will be used? • How will roles be assigned? • What will be said about roles?
Multiple abilities and status treatments • What multiple abilities will be needed? • What will be said about them?	Norms • What norms will be the focus? • What will be said about them?
Group Work: Delegate Authority and Deepen Discourse	
To get started • What actions and interventions might be needed?	Group work skills • What actions and interventions might be needed?
Multiple abilities and status treatments • What actions and interventions might be needed?	Assessing and deepening discourse • What actions and interventions might be needed?
Wrap-Up: Bring to Life What You Value	
Content debrief • What will students share/present? • What will the teacher share/present?	Group work skills • What will students share/present? • What will the teacher share/present?
Multiple abilities and status treatments • What follow-up is needed to the orientation and the observations during group work?	Individual and group accountability • How will students be held accountable for their work? • As a group? • As individuals?

Fig. 6.3. Template for thinking through a group lesson (adapted from TDG [n.d.])

are left with a lot to make sense of after their teaching is finished.

What should a teacher focus on after instruction? Sometimes an event clearly pulls a teacher's attention. Perhaps a teacher needs to work through a group's novel method that seems to work but does not quite make sense. A whole lesson may not have gone the way a teacher anticipated. Maybe none of the groups made any productive headway on the problem; maybe some did but others were mired in trouble. Such events lead to the need to develop a recovery plan for the content or the social environment of the classroom. A teacher may be concerned about a particular student or group of students. Or maybe the collaborative learning strategies have not been yielding the shifts in classroom activities as quickly as a teacher had hoped.

In any case, teachers should take stock of how they met the *mathematical goals* of the lesson:

• What evidence exists that students understood key ideas of the lesson?

• What key teacher questions seemed to support student understanding?

• What misconceptions emerged?

• What ideas from today need to be revisited in the next lesson?

- What kind of mathematical smartness did this activity bring out?

Likewise, they can reflect on their *social goals* for the classroom:

- What was the tone of the classroom today?

- Were students feeling positive about their learning?

- What norms seemed to be working well?

- Which norms need more explicit attention to make this a more productive learning environment?

- Were any problematic status issues in play?

Finally, teachers can go through their roster and do a mental check of how *each student* is making sense of key ideas:

- How was each student smart today?

- Who seems to be understanding the key ideas well?

- Who needs support in getting a handle on key ideas?

- Who needs support on learning to be a student (organization and participation)?

- Who needs to be heard more in the next lesson?

If the same students cause concern day after day, teachers may want to intervene with them before too much time passes by scheduling a conference or calling home.

Classroom life goes by quickly, and teachers often do not have adequate time to make sense of the relationships between instructional choices and outcomes. Teachers new to collaborative learning find it less overwhelming if they focus on a few goals for their teaching. Some examples of goals for a beginner to these methods:

- Getting students to justify their thinking in small-group and whole-class settings

- Remembering to answer only group questions, because this is vital to fostering interdependence

- Getting all students to participate in class, whether during small-group or whole-class discussions

- Creating a safe learning environment where students feel comfortable sharing partially worked-out solutions or errors

By focusing on a few goals to start, teachers will find that this complex practice, linking the social and the mathematical, can grow over time. The social and mathematical goals are intricately related. The social goal is getting students to talk to each other productively, which requires authentically growing their sense of confidence as mathematical thinkers. The mathematical goal is to deepen their thinking, which requires them to talk to each other about their ideas.

Summary

This chapter focused on the teacher's role before, during, and after instruction in an equitable collaborative learning environment. To be effective in these settings, teachers need to reconceptualize their work. Instead of viewing their job as moving through a sequence of curricular topics, teachers should aim for developing enduring mathematical understandings.

Planning focuses on figuring out what is important to teach and its relationship to other content students have learned. Using a planning tool such as the *Thinking Through a Lesson Protocol*, teachers can anticipate students' confusion and think about key questions to assess student understanding. Figure 6.3 offers a template for writing up a lesson that combines TTLP concepts with complex instruction.

During class time, teachers do more than present ideas and guide students toward the completion of work. Once students are involved in a collaborative task, teachers circulate and monitor students' work, using the norms, routines, and strategies discussed in chapter 5. They aim to support students' productive mathematical discourse, as in vignette 4. They survey the different strategies students use and they figure out how to select and sequence them during a whole-class discussion to make important mathematical connections.

After the lesson, teachers can use many strategies to reflect on a lesson and respond accordingly in later ones. Teachers can take stock of the social and mathematical standing of the class as a whole, as well as size up individual students' progress and participation.

To be sure, implementing effective and equitable collaborative learning is an ambitious task. Teachers must make sense of and keep track of a great deal. In the next chapter, I discuss how teacher collaboration can support this goal.

Strength in Numbers of Teachers: Collaboration with Colleagues

Because equitable mathematics teaching and group work require different norms for teaching and learning, it is hard for a single teacher to effectively implement these changes working alone. Students recognize—and often resist—new norms introduced by an idiosyncratic teacher, knowing that the following semester or year they will revert to traditional instruction prevailing elsewhere in their school.

In this chapter, I share some lessons I have learned about how colleagues can work together to create equitable mathematics classrooms, highlighting effective collaborative strategies. These strategies include *observing in each other's classrooms, coplanning, consulting,* and *creating common language* and *common structures* across classrooms. The first three strategies describe ways of working together. The last two strategies are teaching practices that can succeed only if mathematics teachers coordinate their teaching practices across classrooms. The strategies are vital because they ease students' transitions over their years in a school.

Benefits of Productive Collaborations

Collaboration among faculty matters for both teachers and students for several reasons, which I explain in the following sections.

Why Working with Colleagues Matters for Students

I summarized some research on equitable departments and classrooms in table 2.1. In the public imagination, equity is something that individual teachers accomplish. Popular films such as *Stand and Deliver* and *Freedom Writers* show heroic teachers bucking the system to raise student achievement in troubled urban schools. Although individual teachers certainly matter, systemic issues play a significant role in equitable mathematics teaching. Put another way: a single teacher does not constitute all of a student's mathematics education. The opportunity gaps students encounter sometimes arise in all the movement across teachers. During their secondary schooling, students often have eight or more mathematics teachers, all of whom create learning environments, communicate mathematical values, and make consequential judgments about students' mathematical competence. If these conditions vary wildly from year to year, students can feel lost in all the movement.

Educational research supports the idea that equity, in its most important sense, is not simply the accomplishment of an individual teacher. Rather, it is the collective accomplishment of teachers and leaders working together with a common purpose. In high schools, researcher Valerie Lee and her colleagues have investigated the circumstances that support equitable achievement (Lee and Smith 1996). To find such achievement, they looked for schools in which students' demographic background variables (among them, race and socioeconomic status) did not strongly predict curricular attainment level. Schools that have achieved equitable outcomes share identifiable traits: they have a rigorous common curriculum and a strong organizational push for students to enroll in challenging courses. An individual teacher cannot accomplish either of these things. Both require a collective approach.

I have studied departments that organize in this way. They create broader learning environments that help students feel more positive about their mathematics classes in general. The students engage in deep conversations about the content and learn how to persist with difficult problems. Math is not something that is simply an obstacle in their schooling, something to "get through." It becomes a way of looking at the world, a tool they find applicable to their life. In other words, students start to see themselves in the mathematics and are pushed to learn the content more deeply. The success they experience in learning challenging ideas contributes to their overall sense of academic competence and opens up their educational possibilities.

Why Working with Colleagues Matters for Teachers

Setting one's sights on changing teaching practice is an ambitious task. Once teachers have thought carefully about learning and equity, going back to conventional teaching methods is hard. I have yet to meet a teacher who enters the profession to contribute to societal inequities or to limit students' opportunities. At the same time, figuring out new ways of teaching is an intellectual and emotional challenge.

When I talk to teachers who work in collaborative environments, they report several professional benefits. First, they appreciate the support that they get from having like-minded colleagues who listen thoughtfully and empathetically as they share challenges and successes. Teaching can be an isolating profession, with most substantial feedback coming from students. When students push back on changes, a lone teacher without supportive colleagues propping up the effort faces a challenging endeavor. Second, teachers report a sense of accountability when they try things out with their colleagues that they would not feel comfortable doing on their own. In the same way that meeting a friend to exercise increases the likelihood of sticking to the regimen, knowing that somebody else cares about what happens in the classroom motivates teachers to persist in trying out new approaches, even when things get a little rough. There is also the benefit of sharing the workload. If teachers are incorporating groupworthy tasks in their curriculum or making classroom posters with descriptions of group roles, they can divvy up the labor, taking a lead on some efforts and letting colleagues take on others. Finally, just as students' mathematical learning benefits from sharing different strengths and perspectives, so does the work of teachers.

Teachers, like students, find strength in numbers. Like their students, they are often smarter together. Some may have an uncannily astute read on the social world of the classroom. Some understand the math in great depth, some can anticipate many different ways that students will make sense of a concept, while still others are fantastically resourceful at gathering high-quality curriculum materials. When teachers contribute their different assets to a collective effort, everybody's teaching is stronger.

The lesson reflection questions presented at the end of chapter 6 can be answered more thoroughly and with greater confidence when colleagues' perspectives are added to the mix. The value of improvement-focused collegial collaboration is apparent when we look at countries such as Japan, where collegial reflection is central to the teaching profession through the practice of lesson study (Lewis, Perry, and Murata 2006).

Some Ways of Organizing Work with Colleagues

Once teachers have identified colleagues who want to develop equitable collaborative learning structures in their classrooms, they can work together toward that goal. It may just be one partner to start, or it may be a whole department.

To begin with, colleagues should articulate a problem that they want to work on together. Doing so can frame and focus their work and help them communicate what they are doing with administrators or parents. One group of teachers I knew focused on the question, "How can we build a curriculum that shows how our students are smart in mathematics?" Their conversations would always return to this issue, no matter the particular format. Another group started with the question, "How come we have so many students failing freshman mathematics?" After a group inquiry into the causes of the high failure rate and an honest assessment of what they could do about it, they focused on changing their curriculum and updating their teaching practices to help students engage in mathematics. Their question then became, "How do we help our students engage in the mathematics we want them to learn?" Different groups of teachers have different aims for coming together, but whatever the reason, it should be purposeful and not just bureaucratic.

Once the common goal is determined, here are some effective activities teachers can use to deepen their practice together. They include *observing in each other's classrooms, coplanning,* and *consulting.* I describe how teachers I know have used these forms of collaborative work to improve their teaching.

Observing in Each Other's Classrooms

Structuring observations in each other's classrooms is one way to start a teacher collaboration. In the United States, teaching is a private profession, a behind-closed-doors transaction primarily between the adult in charge and students, so this approach may be uncomfortable at first. Most of our experiences with observations typically involve evaluation, so this suggestion represents a transition to restructure them as a learning occasion.

I have found it most successful if teachers organize this work into three phases: a preconference, an observation, and a postconference. This structure may relax a bit over time as teachers grow comfortable with each other's presence, but it helps colleagues shift into the new mode of observation. In the preconference meeting, teachers identify what they want to focus on in their teaching and discuss what they hope to learn from the observations. Teachers can then determine what the observer will look for during the observation and how he will structure his notes. Notes are helpful for jotting down the details of student and teacher talk. The classroom is rich with activity, so choosing a focus will help align the aims of the observer and the observed. Use some of the concepts introduced in earlier chapters and have colleagues observe for status issues, for example, by looking for participation and nonparticipation of students.

During the observation, the observer should play an agreed-upon role. Will he help when students have a question? Or will he sit back and explain that he is just there to watch today? Take notes by using a two-columned table, one labeled "positives" and the other labeled "questions." As a positive, an observer might note, "It was clear that the students knew what to do when they came in the room. They got working right away." As a question, the observer might write, "Did you notice that the four students in the back didn't speak during the whole-class discussion?" Questions, as opposed to criticisms, mark our humility as observers. When we step into a classroom, its history may be invisible during our brief interlude there. The teacher may be making deliberate choices about not pushing the four students in the back for reasons beyond the scope of the one class observation. Of course, the teacher may not realize that the four students were excluded. By posing it as a question, the observer reserves judgment and allows the observed to respond accordingly.

In the postconference, the observer can debrief with the observed teacher. The best approach is often to start by reflecting on the positives before digging into the questions. Just as we want to build from our students' mathematical strengths to support their learning, we want to do the same with our colleagues and ourselves. Starting with the positives is not just a feel-good measure; it is a helpful reminder about what is going well in the classroom and identifies what might be leveraged to address concerns that come up.

Imagine colleagues are working toward greater participation in their math classrooms. The observer notes how well the students discuss problems in their small groups, despite a concern about minimal participation in whole-class discussions. The teacher might use the strength of the substantive small-group discussion to build whole-class discussions. To do this, she might let students know during their group time that they will be called on during the whole-class discussion to share their ideas, giving them the opportunity to practice and anticipate.

This process is iterative, and the observer can switch places with the observed, going through a similar routine of preconference, structured observation, and debrief. Knowing that a plan to change roles is in place helps the observers stay constructive and humble. This structure can be varied to allow multiple teachers into one classroom or a rotation across a larger teacher team. The *positives/question* format for note taking and debriefing can be held constant, no matter how the other arrangements are modified.

> "I know when [complex instruction] has clicked in a classroom when all students are engaged, as seen in body language and as heard in positive interaction between students and teacher. Also, student-to-student talk is respectful and supportive."
>
> —*Ruth Tsu, Retired Mathematics Teacher and Complex Instruction Educator*

Suggested Preliminary Observation

Here I suggest a format for a preliminary observation. One productive observation focuses on the level of mathematical thinking in teachers' classrooms. I have used this topic with both preservice and in-service teachers. To check the mathematical discourse, the observed teacher chooses a lesson in which he or she anticipates a strong whole-class discussion. The observer draws two columns on a piece of paper, one marked "Student Questions" and one marked "Teacher Questions." During the lesson, the observer records all the questions heard in the appropriate column. During the debrief, the observer shares the record with the observed, and they analyze the following together:

- *Frequency* of student questions
- *Frequency* of teacher questions
- *Quality* of questions overall

When looking at questions' quality, teachers can assess what kind of mathematical thinking each question demands. Some questions are *organizational* and necessary for the conduct of the classroom but involve no mathematical thinking ("Do you have your piece of paper out?"). Other questions demand simple *recall* ("What's the definition of *isosceles* again?"). Still others require *procedural thinking* ("How did you get that answer?"), whereas others push on *mathematical habits of mind* ("Can you prove that that's *always* true?") (see chapter 4).

Teachers are often surprised by the ratio of student to teacher questions, as well as the quality of questions in their classroom. Teachers' perception of participation and discourse is sometimes different from reality. This observation technique is a nice way to measure the depth of classroom mathematical discussions and to look for changes over time.

"I've visited a lot of classrooms. When a teacher is intervening and working with a student (or small group of students), it is tempting to focus on the exact exchange. What did the teacher say? What questions did students ask? Instead, I try to study what happens *after* the teacher leaves. Do students turn to each other to clarify what they understand? Do they keep asking questions? Or do they go back to isolated work on the problem? These moments when teachers are actively trying to support a group of students can solidify (or interrupt) status dynamics as much as any other time during the lesson."

—*Phil Tucher, Complex Instruction Educator and Mathematics Educator*

Coplanning

Revamping your teaching toward equitable and meaningful collaborative learning is an ambitious undertaking. Coplanning not only has the benefit of dividing the labor, but when colleagues take the time to check their ideas against some of the concepts developed in this book (*groupworthiness, status, habits of mind*), their own learning of those ideas also has the opportunity to deepen.

Coplanning poses several challenges. Often, the first time through a curriculum, there is not enough time to carefully rethink every lesson. Planning teams can look across a unit, pick a few key lessons to develop more carefully, and use those lessons as a starting point. The key lessons should be the ones that focus on important ideas. Likewise, classes can have different characters. Although two teachers have classes named *algebra*, everything from the time of day to the class size and particular students' personalities make the details of certain activity structures more or less viable. I shared a classroom with a teacher whose class excelled at whole-class discussion. Although I used the same lessons, I knew I could not dwell as long at the start of the lesson because my students did great in small-group work but lost their focus quickly when the lesson launches went on too long. When my colleague and I planned together, I would adapt my lessons to account for this difference. Sometimes, colleagues may simply disagree on the best way to organize a lesson. Perhaps try the lesson in two different formats and report back how students responded to guide future planning decisions. Even better: observe the different choices or take the student work that each class session yields and use these as data to develop insights in the content and the students' understanding of it.

Consulting

When we shift our view of classroom teaching from *clear presentation of ideas* to *creating effective learning environments*, the problem space for our work becomes more complex. Instead of simply looking for the best lessons, teachers need to engage in social engineering specific to their students. How can we increase participation? How do we address issues of status? What about students' competence? How can we support richer mathematical talk in our classrooms? These goals are achieved only with students' cooperation.

Colleagues can help each other think through some of these issues if they are coming from a similar perspective. Teachers who have a troublesome day or a persistent challenge in their classroom can organize a consultation with their colleagues. Such teachers should be prepared to describe the problem and some examples of how they see it playing out in their classroom. Before offering solutions, the listeners can ask questions to gather important details before generating conjectures about the underlying issues. Of course, observations can also help colleagues gather their own information on any of these issues. Because observations are time-intensive and logistically challenging, consultations offer another means to let our colleagues "see" inside our classroom. Again, although sharing expertise and insight is important, so is maintaining a stance of humility, curiosity, and support.

I have observed a useful consultation topic in more than one school setting. In this conversation, which usually takes place around midterm, teachers collect the names of students who are at risk of failing their classes. Teachers bring to the consultation the students' names, the reasons for their low grade, and the interventions the teachers have tried in supporting the students. At a most basic level, teachers can learn from one another's intervention strategies and hear about what has worked with particular students in the past. Teachers can sort out how much of students' difficulties can be attributed to their success at doing school (e.g., attendance, homework submission) and how much has to do with their mathematical learning.

On another level, this consultation potentially harnesses the power of teacher collectivity. In one school, the lists offered evidence of a consistent pattern across classrooms. A disproportionate number of the students had recently transitioned out of sheltered instruction programs designed for English language learners. This development alerted the teachers that they were not doing enough to help students shift into mainstream classrooms. The teachers could then solicit administrators for additional support and resources for this problem.

Consultations are commonplace in many professions. Finding ways to include them in teaching can support teachers' growth and development.

Creating Common Language for Teaching Mathematics

As teachers pay more attention to student competence and listen more closely to students' conversations to assess emerging understandings, I see a shift in their teaching. Teachers' guiding question seems to move from "How should I teach this?" to "How will I help kids think about this?" and eventually to "How will I get different kids with different strengths to talk about this with each other?"

The beauty of mathematics comes, in part, from its logic and order. Understanding how ideas fit together allows students to make sense of what they learn and experience what Theoni Pappas (1989) has called the joy of mathematics. Not all mathematical language lets the concepts shine through, however. When teachers really listen to their students' understanding, they often find the need to change some of the language, even if only transitionally, to help it make more sense. Mathematics educator Liping Ma, for example, has discussed the conceptual trouble that comes from using the term *borrowing* for what is actually *regrouping* in subtraction (Ma 1999). "Borrowing" is a bad metaphor, because when you redistribute tens into the ones column, you never actually give them back. "Regrouping" makes more sense because it explains the breaking of one quantity into its component parts to allow the subtraction algorithm to move forward. Likewise, the term *canceling* has no inherent mathematical meaning and often leads students to believe that numbers magically disappear. The confusion is compounded by the same term being used for the following mathematically distinct procedures:

$$(a) \ \frac{x}{x^2} = \frac{x}{x} \cdot \frac{1}{x} = \frac{\cancel{x}}{x} \cdot \frac{1}{\cancel{x}} = \frac{1}{x}$$

$$(b) \ 2x^2 + 4x + 3y - 4x = 2x^2 + \cancel{4x} + 3y - \cancel{4x} = 2x^2 + 3y$$

In example (a), the mathematical operation involves simplifying an expression by a multiple of 1 (x/x). In (b), opposite terms make a zero. Students often view these forms of canceling as "the same" because, in practice, they strike out these redundant terms on their papers in both cases. Mathematically, however, they are distinct for the reasons I explained. A group of teachers I worked with helped students see this mathematical difference by referring to (a) as "making ones" and (b) as "making zeroes."

Although teachers' adopting this language in their own classes makes sense, students are less confused if they hear the same language across mathematics classrooms in their school. Teachers who cannot coordinate across a whole department might need to flag this as nonstandard language by saying, "You might hear people sometimes call this *borrowing*. But you know I like things to make sense in here, so I prefer the term *regrouping*. That's what we'll call it in my class because . . . ."

Teachers working together can identify this kind of conceptually opaque language and come up with ways to help students manage it effectively.

Creating Common Structures for Teaching

Being a successful mathematics student depends on two things: learning mathematics and being a good student. In practice, we often treat students' grades as if they are assessing only the former, but in mathematics class more than in most other subjects, achievement depends heavily on the latter. Knowing how to turn in homework regularly, study for tests, persist when ideas do not make sense, and keep organized allow students access to ideas that they may not recognize from other parts of their daily life.

Savvy students recognize the ways that school is a game and that every classroom they enter has slight variations on the rules. Secondary students often need to navigate six or more variants of the school game per day. Some teachers want all work done in pen, whereas others insist on pencil. Some teachers are strict about requiring that homework be turned in at the start of class, and others do not require its submission at all. Some teachers require spiral notebooks for notes and work, whereas others want loose-leaf binders or composition books. Teachers vary in how they regulate behaviors such as talking, eating, and tardiness. The potential for students' confusion is compounded by the fact that these rules are not held constant from year to year, or sometimes even from term to term.

Because students' success in mathematics class depends largely on their success in managing the many variations on these rules, schools and departments have increasingly recognized the value of keeping rules constant within and across departments. They recognize that students are more compliant when collectives of teachers keep the rules constant, so students do not have to juggle so many different standards.

Regardless of whether your school is ready to align these practices, perhaps your department or grade-level team is. Brainstorm all the student behaviors your students have difficulty with, everything from putting their names on their papers to turning their homework in regularly. The more that can be standardized across teachers, the fewer variations students need to remember. This standardization also lets teachers support their colleagues' work as well. If a student complains about not knowing her missing assignments in another class, the teacher can remind the student about the common structure (e.g., a homework book or a homework chart) that is a resource for students. The common structures seem to give students a sense of an adult alliance working on their behalf. Just as aligned parents seem to calm children's anxiety, united teachers reassure students that the rules are not arbitrary and serve their success and well-being.

Some examples of structures you might build in common with your colleagues, both within and across your subject areas:

- Homework routines (turning in, recording, displaying)
- Assignment formatting
- Notebook formatting
- Placement of backpacks in the classroom
- "Quick starts"—the expectation that students enter your classroom ready to work
- Testing days
- Testing routines
- Promotion and retention policies
- Rules for calculator use
- Rules for eating, drinking, gum chewing, bathroom, cell phone use

Qualities of Effective Collegial Conversations

I have analyzed hundreds of hours of teacher conversations to uncover which ones seem to support teachers' professional learning. I have identified the following features of productive professional conversations. Use this list as a guide to monitor a group's progress:

- Conversations focus on shared and significant problems of practice (e.g., difficulties that arise in teaching, not simply what to teach next).

- Teachers allow each other adequate time to give attention to issues that arise.

- Teachers trust each other enough to probe each other's stories and revise their interpretation of classroom events.

- Teachers use a consistent and shared set of principles to make sense of problems that arise.

- Teachers consider issues at different time scales. In other words, they are not just talking about what happened today and what should happen tomorrow. They also consider how longer pasts and futures play into the problem at hand.

- Teachers' thinking about curriculum focuses on students' sense making. They ask how students will make sense of mathematical ideas. They use this information to anticipate trouble and identify ways to extend students' thinking.

- Teachers' thinking about students accounts for how *different* students experience an activity or make sense of ideas.

Getting Support for Collaborative Work

The biggest challenge to creating collective structures is that teachers' time is not typically organized to support it. Most secondary teachers have a full schedule of teaching, with one fifty-minute planning period. To work with colleagues, teachers usually spend uncompensated after-school time. The ambitious nature of the teaching model proposed here compounds the challenge of finding that time. If a teacher has 150 student contacts a day, spending one minute per day looking at each student's work requires almost three hours. This simple fact often eludes advocates of more in-depth forms of teaching. The three-hour estimate does not even begin to account for the time needed to plan thoughtful lessons, call home to address concerns, answer parents' e-mail, or write up assessments.

In my view, collective teacher work is ultimately worth the trade-off of time invested. Effective collaborative learning allows you to observe students' thinking during class time, for instance. A successful collegial workgroup allows for the development of many of these time-intensive teaching tools across multiple teachers for multiple years.

Undoubtedly, collective work is best engaged and sustained when administrators and school leaders invest in it by compensating teachers for such work. Most professions are designed to permit collegial interactions; teaching is an unusual exception. Administrators or teacher leaders sometimes have a hard time trusting that teachers' collaborative time will contribute to their larger goals for the school. More than once, I have seen time set aside for teacher collaboration get taken over by administrative tasks such as aligning lesson plans to district standards instead of allowing for the observations and consultations I have described here.

Teachers who are proactive in communicating their purposes to school leadership often have more success in procuring and protecting their collaborative time. Documenting work and linking it to goals that administrators share might also help teachers gain the kind of support that they need. Strong professional communities have been linked to better teaching and student outcomes, and they are worth the investment when they focus on the kind of activities outlined in this chapter.

Ultimately, despite the norms of privacy that pervade teacher culture and the assumptions of our behind-closed-doors independence, we actually *need* our colleagues, regardless of whether we like this fact—or them. Teachers inherently depend on one another because no one of us alone constitutes our students' education. Students move from teacher to teacher, and making that movement coherent is up to us. Acknowledging this interdependence is especially urgent when we consider issues of equity (Horn 2008a).

Summary

Working with colleagues supports the goals of creating equitable collaborative learning environments in individual teachers' classrooms. Students benefit because teachers engage in some of the equitable pedagogical practices described in chapter 2. In effective collaborations, teachers coordinate expectations for students and deeply articulate the curriculum, making more coherent educational experiences for their students. Teachers benefit from the emotional and intellectual support from their colleagues, including sharing colleagues' talents and resources. Collaborations are most effective when teachers focus on a shared problem that they have jointly identified.

Collaboration can take many forms. Most often, teachers work together to coplan lessons, identifying what is important to teach and finding resources for developing groupworthy problems. Intensive collaboration may also include co-observations and consultations around problems of practice. These processes require cultivating common frameworks for thinking about problems of practice and trust among colleagues as they share the details of what is typically private work.

The potential outcomes of intensive collaboration benefit teachers and students. By creating common language for teaching mathematical ideas, teachers make a collective effort to understand student thinking. Students have easier transitions between teachers when their teachers share this language—and even more so when they also share classroom routines and structures.

Effective teacher collaboration has identifiable qualities. Conversations focus on shared and significant problems of practice. Teachers allow each other adequate time to give attention to issues that arise. Teachers trust each other enough to probe each other's stories and revise their interpretation of classroom events. Teachers use a consistent and shared set of principles to make sense of problems that arise. Teachers consider issues at different time scales, not just today and tomorrow. Teachers focus on students' sense making, asking how students will make sense of ideas or representations of mathematical content. They use this thinking to anticipate trouble and identify ways to extend students' thinking. Teachers' thinking about students accounts for how *different* students experience an activity or make sense of ideas.

One of the biggest obstacles to collaboration is time. Typically, secondary schools give teachers little time to plan, let alone collaborate. Administrators can sometimes help teachers procure resources to find that time, particularly if teachers communicate the goals and purposes of their joint work (fig. 7.1).

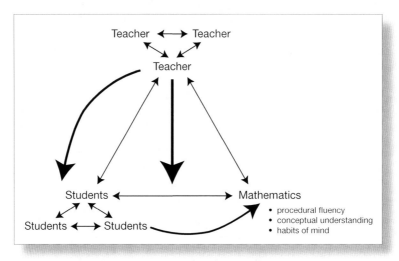

Fig. 7.1. Teachers' colleagues influence their classroom practice.

Putting It All Together: Accounting for the "Dark Matter" in Classroom Life

How do we learn from both research *and* practice? How do we change our teaching in ways that make sense? Change challenges our assumptions and disrupts comfortable routines. How do we translate abstract ideas from research and apply them to the complex environment of a classroom? In this book, I have tried to bring together ideas from research with wisdom and exemplars from practice. Nonetheless, understanding how to usefully bring these seemingly disparate tools and principles together can stretch us.

In part, this challenge comes from the nature of research. When we study complex environments such as classrooms, we decompose them into their constituent parts. We count things or isolate certain kinds of events, exploring correlations and other kinds of relationships. From these investigations, we glean valuable insights, such as the robust relationship between talking about ideas and deepening conceptual understanding. We see how issues of status measurably influence opportunities to talk. Multiple-ability treatments and status interventions can support equal-status interactions (Cohen and Lotan 1995). Over time, with enough instruction that maintains such interactions, achievement differences between student groups can narrow or even disappear (Boaler and Staples 2008). Assessments that focus students on learning increase motivation and achievement (Black et al. 2004). We see time and again that when teachers work collectively to improve instruction, students benefit (Bryk et al. 2010).

As the field of education accumulates these lessons, we say them with more confidence. But a problem remains: how are teachers to take these findings and build their work around them? Research illuminates the significance of these components of practice, yet the challenge of working them into something whole remains.

Sociologist Emanuel Schegloff (1995) imagined the resulting gap between the experienced, messy wholeness and the rigorously examined, neatly dissected components of the social world as a form of dark matter. Dark matter is the substance hypothesized by astronomers to account for differences between theoretical and empirical measurements of the mass of the universe. In the physical universe and the social world, we seek to understand intricate systems by breaking them down into discernible pieces. Inevitably, key aspects of phenomena are left unaccounted for. As people who inhabit the entirety of the classroom, teachers are sometimes left unsatisfied with what researchers report. These components, in isolation, do not reflect our experience and therefore are difficult to use to meaningfully guide our actions. We typically act in the world responding to wholeness, using situational logic, drawing on our knowledge of the culture and history of people, places, and events. We do not, as my student reminded me, live on the "AVERAGE." Teachers may say, "I can see status. I understand that I need to address it. But I can't get status treatments to work in my classroom."

Because my understanding of collaborative learning comes from my work as a researcher, practitioner, and educator, I am sympathetic to this dissatisfaction. I devoted this chapter to bringing together findings of research with the wisdom of practice—what I have learned from observing, using, and teaching pedagogies for collaborative learning. The research that best captures such knowledge comes from Magdalene Lampert's (2003) *Teaching Problems and the Problems of Teaching*. Large-scale research does not substantiate the recommendations I offer in this chapter to the same extent as it does in the earlier chapters in this book. Nonetheless, going from my experience, I believe these recommendations will help people in classrooms move toward the goal of bringing students and mathematics together meaningfully. To me, these practices constitute an important part of the dark matter of classroom life.

Five Practices to Help Change Teaching

When teachers face bringing new ways of teaching into their classroom, I find two major categories of trouble.

The first involves complications in making *adaptations* to teaching practices to suit the setting they are in. These challenges can be structural, such as figuring out how to "put work in the middle" when students' desks are slanted and cannot be lined up to make a usable center when they collaborate. These challenges can also involve the classroom's particular composition. How do you foster collaborative norms when you have three autistic students and no resource support? I have seen teachers contend with these situational challenges inventively, but these obstacles demand creative improvisations to meet the goals of effective collaborative learning.

The other category of trouble comes from *coordinating* new teaching strategies with existing structures and practices. A teacher can manage to follow all the guidelines for collaborative learning in this book, but if the instruction in small-group learning does not jibe with the rest of the learning environment, the implementation will not be as effective. For instance, a teacher seeking to foster positive interdependence during collaborative learning time must avoid invidious comparisons across students. Asking aloud in a moment of frustration why Juan is not more organized like Juanita might not be wise, unless you want Juan to resent Juanita for being a teacher's pet. As discussed in chapter 5, classroom activities that emphasize competition may also send mixed messages about the value of cooperation.

So what is a teacher—or better yet, a team of teachers—to do? In the following sections, I offer five practices that I have seen help teachers undergoing changes in their teaching approaches to manage the transitions. These practices reside in the connective tissue of the classroom—the stuff that holds the parts together—with a focus on relationships, trust, and the other essential intangibles of teaching.

Listen Carefully

Systematically studying listening is hard, yet most teachers recognize the complexity of effective listening. One of the first things I learned as a student teacher was not to write down a student's contribution on the board until he actually finished saying it. Presuming a correct answer is too easy, and clever students will draw out their responses in the hope that the teacher will inadvertently feed it to them by writing down what they are supposed to say.

> "Teachers need to be present when they are interacting with kids. But they also need to be present when they are standing in the shadows. It's easy to think that teaching is going on only when you are talking to kids. But it's happening when you are listening, too."
> —*Laura Evans, Complex Instruction Educator, Mathematics Teacher, and Coach*

The challenge of listening increases with higher-level questions demanding interpretation, justification, and generalization. When people first make sense of new ideas, they do not always speak in fully formed sentences. This issue is only amplified when learners are speaking in a second language. A fundamental question for listening is this:

> *How do teachers interpret emerging ideas in ways that are true to students'* meaning, *instead of presuming we know what they mean on the basis of our grasp of the subject matter?*

I take you now to an example of listening in action. In Courtney Cazden's excellent 2001 book *Classroom Discourse*, the author illustrates the nuance needed for effective listening, drawing on an example from Magdalene Lampert's classroom.

Lampert's students were given four sets of numbers. They were asked to state the rule that transformed the first number into the second:

8 − ?	4
4 − ?	2
2 − ?	1
0 − ?	0

Here is an excerpt of the discussion that shows careful listening on the part of the teacher:

1   *Ellie:*   Um, well, there were a whole bunch of—a whole bunch of rules you could use, use, um, divided by two—and you could do, um, minus one half.

2   *Lampert:*   And eight minus a half is?

3   *Ellie:*   Four. *[A gasp arose from the class.]*

4   *Lampert:*   You think that would be four. What does somebody else think? I started raising a question because a number of people have a different idea about that. So let's hear what your different ideas are, and see if you can take Ellie's position into consideration and try to let her know what your position is. Enoyat?

5   *Enoyat:*   Well, see, I agree with Ellie because you can have eight minus one half and that's the same as eight divided by two or eight minus four.

Lampert continues getting students to air their ideas about the rule and about Ellie's unusual proposal. After more than twenty turns of talk, Lampert explains, "Okay. Let's um . . . one of the things that is kind of a convention in mathematics is that when we just talk about numbers and we don't associate them with any object or group of objects, . . . the symbol means half of one whole. So . . . if you were gonna communicate with the rest of the world who uses mathematics, they would take this [*pointing to the expression "8-½" on the chalkboard*] to mean eight wholes minus one half of a whole. OK? Ellie?"

Eventually, Ellie explains, "That's what I meant, but I just couldn't put it in there, but that's what was in my mind."

Students' emergent thinking will often not be presented in well-polished academic language. Nonetheless, teachers need to hear the thinking behind the imperfect speech. Lampert's response in turn 4 indicates that she hears something more than an incorrect response in what Ellie has said. Lampert, of course, knows that eight minus one-half equals seven and a half, yet she recognizes that this is more than a miscalculation on Ellie's part. She recognizes that there is something to learn about the way we talk about fractions as either a quantity (one-half) or an operator on quantities (one-half of a collection of things). Lampert's careful listening and eventual resolution to Ellie's confusion drew on Lampert's situational knowledge of her students and the mathematics she was teaching.

In small-group settings, not listening carefully can inadvertently exacerbate status problems. If we imagine Lampert simply taking a corrective stance on Ellie's contribution, Ellie's underlying logic would never be revealed. Ellie might be viewed by herself and others as having given an incorrect answer, which in turn may have affected her academic standing in the class. Instead, Lampert's response maintains Ellie as a positive contributor to the class discussion. By building constructively on Ellie's response, Lampert increases the likelihood that Ellie will continue to participate, in both the whole-class and small-group settings. This participation, which allows her to air her own thinking, will in turn deepen her own understanding of the content.

Watch Your Pace

In the United States, most secondary class sessions last between forty-five and sixty minutes. Focusing on big mathematical ideas, developing habits of mind, and using collaborative learning structures may at first slow teachers' progress through the curriculum. This is where the distinction between *covering a topic* and *teaching a topic* becomes invaluable. As I described in chapter 1, we have ample evidence that just because a teacher presents content does not mean students have learned it, let alone learned it well.

Pace refers to more than the rate at which a class moves through the curriculum. It also describes the tempo of interaction. One of the best-known examples of pace in teaching comes from research on *wait time*. Science educator Mary Budd Rowe found that teachers typically wait one second or less for students to reply to questions (Rowe 1974). When teachers waited for three seconds or more, especially after a student response, she found pronounced changes in students' use of language and logic. Increased wait time influenced teacher talk as well. The slower pace allowed teachers to better develop ideas in a lesson, increase the number of cognitively complex questions, and increase the use of student responses in their teaching.

The issue of pace relates to the example from Lampert's classroom. If the focus had been on covering her topic, Lampert would have served that goal more expediently by correcting Ellie and moving forward in her lesson. Because Lampert focused on working with students' mathematical thinking, this teaching goal necessitated a slower pace. Listening and pace are thus deeply related. If teachers rush through lessons, they deny students the opportunity to assimilate ideas—and they deny themselves the opportunity to make sense of student thinking.

Because of its connection to sense making, pace is deeply related to valuing multiple abilities. When lessons are hurried and coverage is the goal, the most valuable student contributions are those that are quick and accurate. To truly value different mathematical smarts, teachers need to listen, consider, and invite other kinds of contributions.

Connect to Students

A major aim of this approach to collaborative learning is to increase the quality and distribution of classroom participation. In addition to changing the pace of lessons, teachers can encourage wider participation by building relationships with students. It is a human truth that we are more willing to take risks when we trust that our effort will be received with kindness and understanding. Making positive connections to students engenders this trust and increases students' willingness to think aloud and contribute mathematically. This may be particularly true for immigrant students, who often feel more trepidation in an unfamiliar culture (Suarez-Orozco 2009).

Relationship building is often viewed as an intangible teacher skill that cannot be taught. I disagree. In my work as a teacher educator, I have learned that there are concrete practices that positively connect teachers and students. They have in common that they express a stance of warmth, acceptance, and curiosity.

Here are some examples of connecting practices. Not everybody needs to use all of them, but incorporating even a few may improve teachers' connections to students. Choose the ones that you can do authentically. Adolescents do not kindly abide phoniness.

Greet students when they arrive.

Students sometimes enter math class apprehensive. A warm hello upon their arrival, particularly at the start of the year, can let them know that this class is a welcoming place. Teachers often neglect greeting their students because they need the time between classes to clean up and prepare. If you cannot stand at the door and say hello to your students, at least look up from your desk as they enter the room to welcome them.

Learn students' names.

For some teachers, learning students' names comes quite naturally. For others, it is a painful struggle. Secondary teachers may have more than 150 student contacts per day. Even so, helping students feel seen and valued is important. Facilitating conversations, fostering positive interdependence, or assigning competence to students who are anonymous is difficult. Learn what your students prefer to be called and how to pronounce their names correctly. Use seating charts and name cards, put photos in your grade book—do what you can to learn students' names. Nothing makes students feel more invisible than when a teacher is obviously avoiding saying their name aloud. (I know this from personal experience.) If pronunciation challenges you, simply let them know. Make it your problem, not theirs. "My job is to say it right by winter break! You're going to have to help me practice. Be sure to correct me if I get it wrong."

Send home "good news" e-mails or postcards.

Too often, the only time parents hear individually from teachers is when trouble arises. If you have a class with students who have a history of academic difficulties, making positive first contact with families is especially wise. Early in the term, devote an hour or two after school to phone home, introduce yourself, ask parents or guardians the best way to reach them, and let them know how much you look forward to having their student in class. If possible, you can let them know when events such as Back-to-School Night happen or how they can get missing homework if their student is absent. The goal is to open the lines of communication *before* any difficulties arise.

Be prepared to take notes. These conversations often give you valuable information. On the most basic level, you can identify wrong numbers in the school directory and find out the families' preferred mode of communication. Parents might also share concerns they have. They may alert you to big issues your students' families are contending with, such as a new divorce or prolonged illness.

Follow up on this contact, particularly with students who lack mathematical confidence, by letting parents know when their students have done well. Perhaps they have made progress on an issue of concern, like turning in homework regularly, or perhaps they did exceptionally well on an assignment. Once students enter secondary school, parents typically lose contact with teachers, but they do not usually lose an interest in seeing their children succeed. Kudos from you can help support your students' positive experiences in your classroom and make them feel valued in your classroom.

Find out something about them.

Students report liking school better when their teachers care about them. This does not mean that teachers need to become surrogate parents or social workers. This means that students want to be seen as the burgeoning individuals that they are coming to know themselves.

Again, when teachers have upwards of 150 students a year, getting to know something unique about each one may seem difficult. Some students—often ones with high social status—are quite vocal about their interests or participate visibly in school life. If your attention is spread thin, seeking out information about students might be reserved for the quietest or most reluctant students.

I learned the Weekend Technique from a teacher I knew. On a Friday, he would ask a few individual students what their plans were for the weekend. He would write this information down in his grade book, noting that they were going to the basketball game or visiting their dad. On Monday, he would follow up, asking, "How was the game?" or "What'd you do with your dad?" He reported that doing so had a profound effect on his students' sense of belonging in his classroom.

Sometimes, our concern for students lies beyond the reach of the Weekend Technique. Most schools keep cumulative folders of students' academic progress. I have often found it valuable to take the time to read up on students' academic backgrounds to better understand their challenges in my class. Some, I learn, have transferred schools every year that they have been in school or even have had substantial gaps in their enrollment. As a result, they are reluctant to invest in their relationships with me or other students. Sometimes, they have been transferred out of special programs, such as language immersion academies or special education, and have lost critical support with no transition plan. This information can help me advocate for them with parents or counselors to get the resources they need.

Have Acceptance of and High Expectations for Students

Complex instruction is a strengths-based approach to teaching students. As teachers, we create learning environments that highlight and value students' competencies, building on these to support their mathematical learning. Sometimes, students arrive in our classrooms with issues that obscure their strengths to their peers—and even from us as teachers. For instance, one student might arrive in your algebra class with a lot of curiosity but a tenuous grasp on multiplication. Another student may come to school noticeably unwashed. Yet another might be prone to rude outbursts.

I have had all three of these hypothetical students in my classrooms. Because a primary goal of collaborative learning is to foster positive interdependence, these students have challenged that goal in different ways. Although many examples exist of students who might be difficult for others to value in a collaborative setting, I will draw on my own experiences to illustrate how teachers can accept challenging students while holding them to high expectations.

The first student, who has a significant gap in her mathematical background, may have a hard time participating in equal-status interactions with her peers. Because the student doesn't know the answer to 4×6, assigning her competence in a way that other students will accept will be a challenge, particularly if they are all fluent in multiplication. As a teacher, it behooves you to look hard at her work to find strengths to publicly recognize and build upon, modeling acceptance of her as a contributor of ideas. At the same time, she needs to have high expectations placed upon her. You might choose to pull her aside and praise her curiosity. Let her know the ways that you recognize her potential while constructing a plan to help her become proficient with multiplication through the resources in your school and community. A meeting with her parents or guardians, letting them in on the arrangement and communicating what is at stake for her future, might be a good idea.

With the second student, a child might arrive at school a bit gamy for a number of reasons. Unfortunately, hygiene becomes an issue in collaborative settings. Other students may want to avoid close contact with him. Teachers, as adults, need to accept students as worth teaching despite an unsavory appearance. At the same time, teachers can communicate greater expectations for self-care, even if through another adult in the school. I was fortunate to have taught in schools that had part-time nurses on staff to whom I could refer students to for this discussion. I was concerned that students might feel self-conscious knowing that I thought they had inadequate cleanliness, so I could write a referral and the student would be called in and advised without knowing who suggested the meeting. In other settings, this conversation may more appropriately fall to counselors.

Such interventions seem beyond the scope of this book but need consideration when you seek to get students to work together respectfully.

Likewise, a student who lashes out at her peers challenges the goal of civil mathematical discourse and positive interdependence in a small-group setting. Feeling accepting of a student who makes others cry is, admittedly, hard. When reasonable effort on my part to curb the student's temper failed to yield results, I sought the help of the counseling office. There, my student was helped with regular counseling on anger-management strategies. For some days, she and I agreed that her working on her own was best, but I made sure to let her know that my expectation was for her to be a good collaborator. Over time, she became a positive contributor in her small group and in the whole class.

A theme runs through these examples that applies to any student who challenges you as a teacher: a need to constantly distinguish between what may be off-putting about a student as a person and his or her ability to learn mathematics. If you recall the principles for equitable teaching, students who present with challenging academic or personal issues often do not get the same opportunities to learn in school as other students. They, too, can be pushed to learn mathematics more deeply. Other students will not be able to accept them as collaborators, though, without your modeling and facilitation.

Model a Stance of Humility and Courage

Trying out new teaching approaches inevitably brings heightened uncertainty. Teacher–researcher Ruth Heaton chronicled her own journey from using traditional to progressive mathematics teaching practices. She eloquently described a persistent state of difficulties and frustration when things often did not go as she expected (Heaton 2000). As she recounts, she felt caught between the old and the new.

Part of Heaton's shift involved moving from a view of teaching as the effective presentation of ideas toward a view of teaching as responsive improvisation. This shift requires openness to what arises, a change that can feel like a loss of control, something that Heaton and many other teachers who have sought to transform their teaching have reported. Presenting oneself as an authority figure to a roomful of adolescents while embracing the uncertainty of a new teaching is not easy.

Once again, I return to Magdalene Lampert, a scholar of mathematics teaching. Lampert describes trying to cultivate in her students a stance of "humility and courage" in their mathematical thinking. By this, she means that they should have the *humility* to listen to others and change their mind about their ideas, while showing the *courage* to state their ideas and stand their ground if they are not convinced by others' arguments.

Teachers who are shifting their teaching can model this stance in their ventures into new forms of teaching. On the one hand, they should have the humility to stop and revise a lesson—mid-class if needed—when their mathematical and social goals have been badly derailed. On the other hand, they should have the courage to persevere, even in the face of pushback by students. I have often heard students protest the notion of explaining their thinking. You can best meet this objection with a caring response, such as, "I want you to really understand this, and I find that when you can explain something, you will know it better and remember it later." Humility and courage are valuable for both teachers and their students.

Summary

Learning to teach in new ways can seem like a daunting task. No one practice or principle in this book will transform your teaching; the whole classroom truly is greater than the sum of its parts. Teachers can more effectively navigate the complexity of trying out new methods by paying close attention to how they adapt new practices to their classrooms, making sure that the improvised versions still maintain the original intent. Likewise, they will have to consider how new practices coordinate with existing practices in their classrooms. Students will pick up any contradictory messages and gravitate to the ones that are more comfortable.

I propose that five practices, in particular, will support the work of adaptation and coordination. Teachers must learn to *listen* carefully to students, with a focus on students' meaning. Issues of *pace*, both at the level of interaction and through the curriculum, have profound influences on teachers' and students' sense-making opportunities. To elicit students' thinking, teachers need to *connect with students:* cultivate relationships, contributing to students' sense of connection and belonging. Likewise, even difficult students demand a level of *acceptance* from their teachers. Accepting students does not mean abandoning *high expectations,* whether social or mathematical. Finally, teachers taking on new practices have an opportunity to model *humility and courage,* an attitude that benefits teacher learning of new pedagogies as much as it benefits students' learning of mathematics.

Learning is not the same as achievement. Achievement gaps often reflect opportunity gaps. All students can be pushed to learn mathematics more deeply. Students need to see themselves in mathematics—and I hope that you can help them to do so.

Resources

Mathematics Teaching

Connecting Mathematical Ideas: Middle School Video Cases to Support Teaching and Learning, by Jo Boaler and Cathy Humphreys (2005). This book provides models for leading productive mathematical discussions by using rich problems, with commentary by the teacher (Humphreys) and essays connecting to research (Boaler). The text comes with two CD-ROMs of video from Humphreys's classroom.

Elementary and Middle School Mathematics: Teaching Developmentally (7th Edition), by John A. Van de Walle, Karen S. Karp, and Jennifer M. Bay-Williams (2010). This book nicely outlines how students' conceptual understanding develops in major topics in elementary and middle school mathematics. It provides good sample problems along with ideas about how to use them in classrooms to engage students' thinking.

Fostering Algebraic Thinking (1999) and *Fostering Geometric Thinking* (2007), by Mark Driscoll and colleagues. In these two volumes, Driscoll focuses on big ideas in algebra and geometry for grades 6–10. Both books describe habits of mind characteristic to each domain and provide rich problems, along with productive ways to help students think them through.

Teaching Math: A Grade 9–12 Video Library, the Annenberg Foundation (1996), online at http://www.learner.org/resources/series34.html. A collection of classroom video showing teachers and students working with mathematical ideas. Includes several support resources. Check out the video *Group Test* to see a teacher using this complex instruction method in his advanced algebra classroom.

"Five 'Key Strategies' for Effective Formative Assessment," by Dylan Wiliam, *National Council of Teachers of Mathematics Research Brief.* Reston, Va.: NCTM, 2007. A concise, four-page document that outlines important assessment strategies that have been shown to support productive and equitable outcomes in mathematics classrooms. Downloadable at http://www.nctm.org/news/content.aspx?id=11474.

Rich Mathematical Activities

EQUALS Investigations Units Lawrence Hall of Science, University of California, Berkeley (1994). http://lawrencehallofscience.org/equals/EQbkInvest.html. Five spiral-bound units available in English and Spanish designed to provide middle school teachers (grades 6–9) with rich curricula on important topics. The problems are engaging and have multiple points of entry. The units lend themselves to collaborative learning environments.

Balanced Assessments task bank. http://balancedassessment.concord.org/. The Balanced Assessment in Mathematics Program, from the Harvard Graduate School of Education, developed a large collection of innovative mathematics tasks for grades K–12, along with scoring rubrics for assessing student performance. The library of more than 300 mathematics assessment tasks developed during the project remains freely available through this website. Teachers may use these materials in their own classrooms at no cost.

About Teaching Mathematics: A K–8 Resource (2nd Edition), by Marilyn Burns. This classic book offers activities and resources for teachers who want to incorporate richer mathematical tasks in their classrooms. The tasks are sorted by topic and supported with commentary to help teachers think deeply about the content, along with guidance for how to structure students' explorations.

The Math Forum. http://mathforum.org/. A website that has rich problems, a feature called Ask Dr. Math, a teacher-to-teacher network, and professional development. Hosted by Drexel University.

Complex Instruction

Designing Groupwork: Strategies for the Heterogeneous Classroom (2nd Edition), by Elizabeth Cohen (1994). Cohen's classic book introduces the theory behind complex instruction, along with classroom examples. The text draws on years of research in laboratories and classrooms and discusses strategies and provides tools for bringing cooperative learning into different settings.

Complex Instruction Website, hosted by Stanford University. http://cgi.stanford.edu/group/pci/. A place to explore some of the people and projects behind complex instruction. This resource has links to curricula in different subject areas as well as classroom video examples.

References

Allexsaht-Snider, Martha, and Laurie E. Hart. "'Mathematics for All'—How Do We Get There?" *Theory into Practice* 40, no. 2 (2001): 93–101.

Aronson, Joshua. "The Threat of Stereotypes." *Educational Leadership* 62, no. 3 (2004): 14–19.

Banilower, Eric R., P. Sean Smith, Iris R. Weiss, and Joan D. Pasley. "The Status of K–12 Science Teaching in the United States: Results from a National Observation Study." In *The Impact of State and National Standards on K–12 Science Teaching*, edited by D. W. Sunal and E. L. Wright, pp. 83–122. Greenwich, Conn.: IAP, 2006.

Black, Paul, Christine Harrison, Clare Lee, Bethan Marshall, and Dylan Wiliam. "Working Inside the Black Box: Assessment for Learning in the Classroom." *Phi Delta Kappan* 86 (September 2004): 9–21.

Boaler, Jo. *Experiencing School Mathematics: Traditional and Reform Approaches and Their Influence on Student Thinking*. New York: Routledge, 2002.

Boaler, Jo, and James Greeno. "Identity, Agency, and Knowing in Mathematical Worlds." In *Multiple Perspectives on Mathematics Teaching and Learning*, edited by Jo Boaler, pp. 171–200. Stamford, Conn.: Ablex, 2000.

Boaler, Jo, and Cathy Humphreys. *Connecting Mathematical Ideas: Middle School Video Cases to Support Teaching and Learning*. Portsmouth, N.H.: Heinemann, 2005.

Boaler, Jo, and Megan Staples. "Creating Mathematical Futures through an Equitable Teaching Approach: The Case of Railside School." *Teachers College Record* 110, no. 3 (2008): 608–45.

Bransford, John D., Ann L. Brown, and Rodney Cocking. *How People Learn: Brain, Mind, Experience, and School*. Washington, D.C.: National Research Council, 2000.

Bryk, Anthony S., Penny Bender Sebring, Elaine Allensworth, Stuart Lappescu, and John Q. Easton. *Organizing Schools for Improvement: Lessons from Chicago*. Chicago: University of Chicago Press, 2010.

Burns, Marilyn. *About Teaching Mathematics: A K–8 Resource*. 3rd ed. Sausalito, Calif.: Math Solutions Publications, 2007.

Cazden, Courtney. *Classroom Discourse: The Language of Teaching and Learning*. 2nd ed. Portsmouth, N.H.: Heinemann, 2001.

Cobb, Paul, and Lynn Liao Hodge. "A Relational Perspective on Issues of Cultural Diversity and Equity as They Play Out in the Mathematics Classroom." *Mathematical Thinking and Learning* 4, no. 2–3 (2002): 249–84.

Cohen, Elizabeth G. *Designing Groupwork: Strategies for the Heterogeneous Classroom*. New York: Teachers College Press, 1994.

Cohen, Elizabeth G., and Rachel A. Lotan. "Producing Equal-Status Interaction in the Heterogeneous Classroom." *American Educational Research Journal* 32, no. 1 (1995): 99–120.

———. "Equity in Heterogeneous Classrooms." In *Handbook of Research on Multicultural Education*, edited by James A. Banks and Cherry McGee Banks, pp. 736–52. Hoboken, N.J.: Jossey-Bass, 2003.

Cohen, Elizabeth G., Rachel A. Lotan, Percy L. Abram, Beth A. Scarloss, and Susan E. Schultz. "Can Groups Learn?" *Teachers College Record* 104, no. 6 (2002): 1045–68.

Cuoco, Al, E. Paul Goldenberg, and June Mark. "Habits of Mind: An Organizing Principle for Mathematics Curricula." *Journal of Mathematical Behavior* 15, no. 4 (1996): 375–402.

Delpit, Lisa. *Other People's Children: Cultural Conflict in the Classroom.* New York: New Press, 1995.

Driscoll, Mark. *Fostering Algebraic Thinking: A Guide for Teachers, Grades 6–10.* Portsmouth, N.H.: Heinemann, 1999.

Driscoll, Mark, Rachel Wing DiMatteo, Johanna Nikula, and Michael Egan. *Fostering Geometric Thinking: A Guide for Teachers,* Grades 5–10. Portsmouth, N.H.: Heinemann, 2007.

Flores, Alfinio. "Examining Disparities in Mathematics Education: Achievement Gap or Opportunity Gap?" *High School Journal* 91, no. 1 (2007): 29–42.

Gibbons, Pauline. "Mediating Language Learning: Teacher Interactions with ESL Students in a Content-Based Classroom." *TESOL Quarterly* 37, no. 2 (2003): 247–73.

Gresalfi, Melissa Sommerfeld. "Taking up Opportunities to Learn: Constructing Dispositions in Mathematics Classrooms." *Journal of the Learning Sciences* 18, no. 3 (2009): 327–69.

Gresalfi, Melissa, Taylor Martin, Victoria Hand, and James Greeno. "Constructing Competence: An Analysis of Student Participation in the Activity Systems of Mathematics Classrooms." *Educational Studies in Mathematics* 70, no. 1 (2009): 49–70.

Gutierrez, Rochelle. "Practices, Beliefs, and Cultures of High School Mathematics Departments: Understanding Their Influences on Student Advancement." *Journal of Curriculum Studies* 28, no. 5 (1996): 495–530.

Heaton, Ruth. *Teaching Mathematics to the New Standards: Relearning the Dance.* New York: Teachers College Press, 2000.

Henningsen, Marjorie, and Mary Kay Stein. "Supporting Students' High-Level Thinking, Reasoning, and Communication in Mathematics." In *Lessons Learned from Research,* edited by Judith Sowder and Bonnie Schappelle, pp. 27–36. Reston, Va.: National Council of Teachers of Mathematics, 2002.

Hill, Heather C., Brian Rowan, and Deborah Loewenberg Ball. "The Effects of Teachers' Mathematical Knowledge for Teaching on Student Achievement." *American Educational Research Journal* 42, no. 2 (2005): 371–406.

Horn, Ilana Seidel. "Why Do Students Drop Advanced Mathematics?" *Educational Leadership* 62 (November 2004): 61–64.

———. "Lessons Learned from De-tracked Mathematics Departments." *Theory into Practice* 45, no. 1 (2006): 72–81.

———. "The Inherent Interdependence of Teachers." *Phi Delta Kappan* 89 (June 2008a): 751–54.

———. "Turnaround Students in High School Mathematics: Constructing Identities of Competence through Mathematical Worlds." *Mathematical Thinking and Learning* 10, no. 3 (2008b): 201–39.

Kazemi, Elham. "Discourse That Promotes Conceptual Understanding." *Teaching Children Mathematics* 4 (March 1998): 410–14.

Kelly, Sean, and Julianne Turner. "Rethinking the Effects of Classroom Activity Structure on the Engagement of Low-Achieving Students." *Teachers College Record* 111, no. 7 (2009): 1665–92.

Kilpatrick, Jeremy, W. Gary Martin, and Deborah Schifter, eds. *A Research Companion to "Principles and Standards for School Mathematics."* Reston, Va.: National Council of Teachers of Mathematics, 2003.

Kilpatrick, Jeremy, Jane Swafford, and Bradford Findell, eds. *Adding It Up: Helping Children Learn Mathematics.* Washington, D.C.: National Academies Press, 2001.

Kozol, Jonathan. *Savage Inequalities: Children in America's Schools*. New York: Harper Collins, 1991.

Lampert, Magdalene. *Teaching Problems and the Problems of Teaching*. New Haven, Conn.: Yale University Press, 2003.

Lampert, Magdalene, and Deborah Loewenberg Ball. *Teaching, Multimedia, and Mathematics: Investigations of Real Practice*. New York: Teachers College Press, 1998.

Latour, Bruno. *Science in Action: How to Follow Scientists and Engineers through Society*. Cambridge, Mass.: Harvard University Press, 1997.

Lee, Valerie, and Julia B. Smith. "Collective Responsibility for Learning and Its Effects on Gains in Achievement for Early Secondary School Students." *American Journal of Education* 104, no. 2 (1996): 103–47.

Lewis, Catherine, Rebecca Perry, and Aki Murata. "How Should Research Contribute to Instructional Improvement? The Case of Lesson Study." *Educational Researcher* 35, no. 3 (2006): 3–14.

Lotan, Rachel. "Group-Worthy Tasks." *Educational Leadership* 60, no. 6 (2003): 72–75.

MacLeod, Alexander. "Math Teacher, Call Your Image Consultant!" *Christian Science Monitor*, Jan. 8, 2001.

Ma, Liping. *Knowing and Teaching Elementary Mathematics: Teachers' Understanding of Mathematics in China and the United States*. New York: Routledge, 1999.

Martin, Danny Bernard. *Mathematics Success and Failure Among African American Youth: The Roles of Sociohistorical Context, Community Forces, School Influence, and Individual Agency*. Mahwah, N.J.: Erlbaum, 2000.

———. "Mathematics Learning and Participation as Racialized Forms of Experience: African American Parents Speak on the Struggle for Mathematical Literacy." *Mathematical Thinking and Learning* 8, no. 3 (2006): 197–229.

McLaughlin, Milbrey W., and Joan E. Talbert. *Professional Communities and the Work of High School Teaching*. Chicago: University of Chicago Press, 2001.

Moll, Luis C., Cathy Amanti, Deborah Neff, and Norma Gonzalez. "Funds of Knowledge for Teaching: Using a Qualitative Approach to Connect Homes and Classrooms." *Theory into Practice* 31, no. 2 (1992): 132–41.

Moschkovich, Judit. "Supporting the Participation of English Language Learners in Mathematical Discussions." *For the Learning of Mathematics* 19, no. 1 (1999): 11–19.

Moses, Robert P., and Charles E. Cobb Jr. *Radical Equations: Civil Rights from Mississippi to the Algebra Project*. Boston: Beacon Press, 2001.

Nieto, Sonia, and Patty Bode. *Affirming Diversity: The Sociopolitical Context of Multicultural Education*. 6th ed. Boston: Allyn and Bacon, 2011.

Oakes, Jeannie. *Keeping Track: How Schools Structure Inequality*. 2nd ed. New Haven, Conn.: Yale University Press, 2005.

Oakes, Jeannie, Megan Loef Franke, Karen Hunter Quartz, and John Rogers. "Research for High-Quality Urban Teaching: Defining It, Developing It, Assessing It." *Journal of Teacher Education* 53, no. 3 (2002): 228–34.

Organization for Economic Co-operation and Development (OECD). *Lessons from PISA for the United States: Strong Performers and Successful Reformers in Education*. OECD Publishing, 2011. doi:10.1787/9789264096660, p. 32.

Pappas, Theoni. *The Joy of Mathematics: Discovering the Mathematics All Around You*. San Carlos, Calif.: Worldwide Publishing/Tetra, 1989.

Phelan, Patricia, Ann Locke Davidson, and Hanh Cao Yu. *Adolescents' Worlds: Negotiating Family, Peers, and School*. New York: Teachers College Press, 1997.

Planty, Michael, Stephen Provasnik, and Bruce Daniel. *High School Coursetaking: Findings from "The Condition of Education 2007."* U.S. Department of Education. Washington, D.C.: National Center for Education Statistics, 2007.

Rowe, Mary Budd. "Wait Time and Rewards as Instructional Variables, Their Influence on Language, Logic, and Fate Control." *Journal of Research in Science Teaching* 11 (1974): 81–84.

Schegloff, Emanuel. "Confirming Allusions: Towards an Empirical Account of Action." *American Journal of Sociology* 104, no. 1 (1995): 161–216.

Schoenfeld, Alan H. *Mathematical Problem Solving*. San Diego: Academic Press, 1985.

———. "When Good Teaching Leads to Bad Results: The Disasters of 'Well Taught' Mathematics Courses." *Educational Psychologist* 23, no. 2 (1988): 145–66.

———. "Making Mathematics Work for All Children: Issues of Standards, Testing, and Equity." *Educational Researcher* 31, no. 1 (2002): 13–25.

Smith, Margaret, Victoria Bill, and Elizabeth K. Hughes. "Thinking Through a Lesson: Successfully Implementing High-Level Tasks." *Mathematics Teaching in the Middle School* 14 (October 2008): 132–38.

Spender, Dale. *Invisible Women: The Schooling Scandal*. Chap. 4, pp. 55–56. London: Writers and Readers Publishing Cooperative Society, 1982.

Stein, Mary Kay, Randi A. Engle, Margaret S. Smith, and Elizabeth K. Hughes. "Orchestrating Productive Mathematical Discussions: Five Practices for Helping Teachers Move Beyond Show and Tell." *Mathematical Thinking and Learning* 10, no. 4 (2008): 313–40.

Stevenson, Harold. *The Learning Gap: Why Our Schools Are Failing and What We Can Learn from Japanese and Chinese Education*. New York: Simon and Schuster, 1994.

Stigler, James W., and James Hiebert. *The Teaching Gap: Best Ideas from the World's Teachers for Improving Education in the Classroom*. New York: Free Press, 1999.

Stodolsky, Susan, and Pamela L. Grossman. "Changing Students, Changing Teaching." *Teachers College Record* 102, no. 1 (2000): 125–72.

Suarez-Orozco, Carola, Alyson Pimentel, and Margary Martin. "The Significance of Relationships: Academic Engagement and Achievement among Newcomer Immigrant Youth." *Teachers College Record* 111, no. 3 (2009): 712–49.

Teachers Development Group (TDG). *Designing Groupwork in Mathematics: Institute Journal and Readings*. Portland, Ore.: TDG, n.d.

Treisman, Uri. "Studying Students Studying Calculus: A Look at the Lives of Minority Mathematics Students in College." *College Mathematics Journal* 23, no. 5 (1992): 362–72.

Van de Walle, John A., Karen S. Karp, and Jennifer M. Bay-Williams. *Elementary and Middle School Mathematics: Teaching Developmentally*. 7th ed. Boston: Allyn and Bacon, 2010.

Webb, Noreen. "Task-Related Verbal Interaction and Mathematics Learning in Small Groups." *Journal of Research in Mathematics Education* 22 (November 1991): 366–89.

Wiggins, Grant P., and Jay McTighe. *Understanding by Design*. 2nd ed. Alexandria, Va.: Association for Supervision and Curriculum Development, 2005.